Ketoge

Shortcut to Ketosis- L
Beginners Guide to Over
Recipes w

MW00954473

Jeremy Stone

Elevate Publishing Limited

Contents

For years we were told that fats are bad for us and to be healthy we should eat more carbs. But as our knowledge of science and nutrition advanced, we now know fats aren't as bad as we once thought! This is where the Ketogenic Diet comes in. Scientific studies now show the dangers and risks associated with simple carb diets. At the same time, there are many studies that show the health benefits of a high-fat low-carb diet, including:

- **Increased Energy and Focus**
- **Increased Weight Loss**
- **Lowered Blood Sugar Levels**
- **Decrease in Hunger**
- **Lowered Bad Cholesterol Levels**
- **Reduction in Acne and Skin Inflammation**

After reading several Ketogenic recipe books, I became disappointed because there was so much information that I wanted to know but wasn't included in the books. I found myself researching the nutritional information for each recipe I have been interested in just to make sure I wasn't eating too many carbs.

I wanted to make a Ketogenic recipe book that was helpful not only to beginners thinking about starting the diet, but also to people who have been on it for years, but are looking for cool recipes that had all the macro- and micro-nutrients right there in front of their face. Also, because time is so important, all recipes are sorted by the least amount of time to the longest amount of time to prepare and cook.

This book contains proven tips and Shortcuts on how you can enter Ketosis. You will read straightforward information on the diet, what to expect, and lots of delicious recipes to keep you going.

Work your body into Ketosis and you will find an amazing way to lose weight, gain energy, and stay fit. As with any diet, make sure to consult with a physician before you start.

Also make sure to follow me on Twitter for all the latest news, tips, and more recipes @JeremyStoneEat

Chapter 1

What is the Ketogenic Diet?

If you are anything like me, you've been on diets before and knew that they don't work. They don't work because they take too much willpower to keep it going in the long term. I come from an old school family where you don't leave anything left on the plate. That's how my problem of overeating started, and it affected me my whole life. What makes the Ketogenic Diet work is that it isn't a diet in the traditional sense of the word. There is no calorie counting, no going to bed hungry, no feeling guilty after having a big meal.

The Ketogenic Diet works because it changes how our bodies process energy. This method of eating is not so new and has been around for thousands of years. Unfortunately, modern society is selecting convenience foods loaded with carbohydrates and refined sugars. Today, eating is often done on the run. Convenience is what sells, and manufacturers satisfy consumers' demands. These convenience foods come with preservatives, dyes, added refined sugar, salt, and processed grains. While it may be convenient to our schedule, these foods are not convenient for our body to process.

The Ketogenic Diet may sound complex and technical, but, simply put, this diet is feeding your body foods that it can process more easily. The human body is made to function using food for fuel, which in turn gives us energy. The Ketogenic Diet optimizes this process with the result of more energy.

There are four sources of fuel for the body: carbohydrates, fat, protein, and ketones. Most carbohydrates are grains and sugars that are burned off by the body first, or the excess is stored as fat. Fats are in nuts, seeds, meats, poultry, seafood, dairy, and oils. Protein is in meat, poultry, seafood, legumes, eggs, dairy, processed soy products, nuts, and seeds. Fats and proteins are efficient sources of energy utilized our bodies utilize better than carbohydrates.

But what are ketones? Ketones occur when fat in the body is broken down. The result of a Ketogenic Diet is that fat and ketones become the main source of fuel for the body. The key to eating a Ketogenic Diet is to consume more fats, some protein, and little few carbohydrates. This allows your body enter a state of Ketosis. Once in Ketosis, your body becomes a fat burning machine, and you will start to lose weight quickly. By following this book, you will have a better understanding of the diet and will help you avoid mistakes so that you can enter Ketosis quickly.

Understanding the diet

To reap the health benefits, there needs to be an understanding of how the diet works. So, let's take a look at exactly what a Ketogenic Diet is. Before starting any diet, you need to discuss the benefits and/risks with your doctor. It is important to understand the impact a diet may have on your body and your medical conditions. This will help you choose a diet that will be safe and give optimal results.

Wait, did you say little carbs?

People are often concerned that a lack of adequate carbohydrates could cause an issue. Carbohydrates provide the body with glucose, but proteins can also be converted into glucose for fuel. Additionally, minimizing carbohydrates can decrease fiber in the diet. Fiber, needed for digestive health, can be obtained from other sources such as vegetables. Also, probiotics and fermented foods keep your digestive system running smoothly (literally and figuratively). Eating a Ketogenic Diet is not just eating a low-carbohydrate diet. Rather than counting carbohydrates, consider being aware of your body and how it is responding to the foods you consume. Are you giving yourself the nutrients that you need? A Ketogenic Diet is a change in lifestyle and mindset. Food is a source of fuel. Some foods are more efficient and clean burning fuels, while other foods are eaten to meet a taste. It is possible to eat foods that are good for you and taste good too. Give yourself two weeks for your taste buds to adjust and the sugar cravings to disappear.

Ketogenic vs. Ketoacidosis

Confusion may occur between a Ketogenic Diet and ketoacidosis. Ketosis is when your body uses ketones, rather than glucose, for fuel. Ketoacidosis is a serious medical condition. It can occur in diabetes, alcoholism, long-term starvation, long-term excessive exercise, or with the street drug Ecstasy. These conditions can cause acidic blood levels from an accumulation of ketones in the blood leading to serious health complications. In a healthy individual, prevention of ketoacidosis naturally occurs. The body has normal mechanisms to balance the blood levels. Ketogenic Diets in healthy individuals do not result in ketoacidosis.

Why choose a Ketogenic Diet over another type of diet?

Some diets succeed, and other diets fail. Diets that succeed control hunger. A management of hormones and messengers in the body result from fats and ketones being used for fuel. This management leads to decreased cravings, better food choices and greater weight loss. These benefits are enhanced when the body can burn fat for energy rather than just carbohydrates. If the body uses carbohydrates to convert glucose to energy, blood sugar levels can drop fast. The results are hunger and cravings for sugar and carbohydrates.

On a Ketogenic Diet, drops in blood sugar are minimized. This is because fats and ketones serve as fuel rather than quick-burning carbohydrates. Weight loss is hindered by foods that cause cravings for sugar, salt, and fats. These addictive foods cause over-consumption of food that never give a true feeling of satisfaction. Most often, processed foods are the culprits. On a Ketogenic Diet, these foods can be avoided and so are the resulting junk food cravings and hunger.

Instead of calorie counting, stick to foods found in nature and that are simple to pronounce. Foods such as grains, dairy, and refined sugar cause inflammation in the body. Inflammation hinders weight loss and causes toxins to build up in your body. After starting the Ketogenic Diet, the toxins will be removed, and inflammation will decrease. This will lead to a healthier you.

So how much can I eat?

Before starting a ketogenic meal plan, it's important to know the amounts of macronutrients to consume throughout the day. Macronutrients can be broken down into three major categories (carbs, protein, and fats) and we will discuss each in detail.

Carbs

Currently, the USDA is being pressed with regards to how unhealthy the recommended daily allowance of carbohydrates (225 to 358 grams) can be for someone to ingest. At the moment, people in North America get the majority of their calories from dietary carbohydrates.

It's no wonder we are so sick and overweight. The optimal range for any person looking to achieve ketosis will usually be below 50 grams per day. There are a few ranges from high to low-carb intake that come before ketosis, and it is important to be aware of them to understand the reasons and benefits of a ketogenic diet. Below are the different levels of carbohydrate intake and the effects on your body.

150–300+ grams – Dangerous caloric carbohydrate intake

This range of carbohydrates intake is the average range of a normal American. The excessive amount of carb consumption at this level can cause many physical issues and lead to many diseases, such as diabetes and metabolic syndrome. Staying at this level on can lead to the gain of 1.5 pounds of weight gain every year on average.

100–150 grams – The gray zone

This level is the ideal area for maintaining a consistent weight, along with some exercise. This carbohydrate intake level at this range is not ideal to when pursuing weight loss.

50–100 grams – Long term success zone

This range is where insulin production is reduced, and your body begins to burn more fat for energy. By remaining at this level, you can still enjoy many fruits and vegetables and still lose a couple of pounds of body fat per week. Although some carbs at this level are high, some people can still be in Ketosis in this zone. This level of carb intake can realistically be sustained long term.

0–50 grams – Shortcut to Ketosis Zone

Because this book is about achieving Ketosis quickly, this is the level where you want to be at to achieve rapid weight loss on a Ketogenic Diet. However, staying at this level may not be recommended long term as if you are not careful you may deprive your body of healthy fruits and vegetables.

Protein

Protein is essential for weight loss and overall health and wellbeing, which is why the ketogenic diet promotes moderate consumption of protein. It's very important to get enough protein to maintain your muscles, but not too much, as that would kick you out of ketosis. There are many online calculators where you can enter your basic information such as gender and weight to get the exact amounts of nutrients you need in a ketogenic diet.

Protein intake is usually calculated according to a person's weight and activity level. For example, if you weigh 175 pounds and have 30% body fat, and your lean body mass is 122.5 pounds (175 × 0.7), your daily protein intake should be about 86 grams a day (122.5 × 0.7). Another way of calculating your target protein intake is getting 15% to 20% of your total calorie intake from protein. For this, you can use the following formula: calories x (0.15 to 0.2) / 4 = grams of protein.

Fats

You already know that following a ketogenic diet includes a high intake of fat. However, before you assume you can freely eat as much junk food as you want, you need to know that not all fat is created equal.

To become keto-adapted and reach ketosis, you have to increase your intake of healthy fats. The amount of fat you should eat on a daily basis depends on your caloric needs. Ideally, between 70% and 80% of your entire calorie intake during the day should be healthy fats. Here is a formula you can use to get a more specific insight into fat intake: calories x (0.7 to 0.8) / 9 = grams of fat.

Health Benefits

In 1924, Dr. Russell Wilder at the Mayo Clinic designed the Ketogenic Diet as an aid for epilepsy patients. It was Dr. Wilder's idea that this type of diet mirrored the biochemical changes associated with fasting. Earlier treatments identified fasting as a way to control seizures in children and young adults.

Since Dr. Wilder's time, the Ketogenic Diet has been used for epileptic patients when medications don't work. Although originally used for seizure control, additional clinical trials and studies have shown that a diet resulting in ketosis also have an impressive effect on increased weight loss, higher energy levels, and a decrease in hunger. Many people also note a significant increase in mental focus while on the diet.

Dr. Steve Phinney, a doctor with 35 years of studying healthy low-carb diets, found that after six weeks of keto-adaption, an average of 90 grams (3.17 ounces) of fat was burned per hour on his test subjects. If you were eating a diet full of carbohydrates, this fat burn would only be 30 grams (1.058 ounces) per hour (This is how the Ketogenic Diet turns you into a fat burning machine!

Also these noticeable effects, the Ketogenic Diet has several other health benefits that aren't as obvious but are just as important for your long-term health. The first effect is that blood pressure tends to go down. We know that elevated blood pressure is an important risk factor for many diseases but by following the diet, studies have shown that it decrease blood pressure.

Second, studies have found that while on the diet, HDL Cholesterol (the "good" kind) were increased while LDL

Cholesterol (the "bad" kind) were changed lowered to be less dangerous levels. People with diabetes will especially find health benefits from a Keto-based diet, as it has been shown to lower blood sugars and reduce the need for insulin.

The Food List

Now that you have an idea of the Ketogenic Diet is, let's get to the fun part and take a look at what you can eat!

This is by no means an entire inventory, but it will give you a general idea of what you should eat and what you should avoid. Since the diet is triggered by eating fats, let's start out with a sampling of what fats are good for you:

Fats

- Fats should be the largest source of your calories. So, it is important that you are eating the right amount of healthy fats. This includes eating a balanced diet of Omega 6 and Omega 3 fatty acids. Most of your fats should come from saturated and mono-unsaturated fats. These include the following:
- Grass-fed butter, Coconut butter
- Avocado
- Cold pressed oils – Olive, Grape Seed, Coconut
- Ghee
- Nuts – Peanut, Macadamia, Almond
- Some cheeses – Cheddar, Cream Cheese, Goat cheese be careful as some have more carbs than others.

Proteins

When it comes to proteins, you want to stick with anything organic or grass fed. Free range eggs are my personal favorite, as they are cheap and a guilt-free source of protein!

- Beef – Steaks, roast beef, beef stew (if you can find grass- fed beef, it tends to be leaner, but healthier).

- Pork – Sausage, bacon, chops (try to stay away from processed meats)

- Chicken – Breast, thighs, free range is best (If eating a whole chicken, take off the skin as it may contain carbs)

- Fish – Salmon, mackerel, tuna, any fish caught in the wild is preferable (Loaded with healthy Omega 3's)

- Whole Eggs – Again free range is best, I prefer to make it into omelets

- Nut Butter – Peanut, Almond, Macadamia, (Get natural butter, has good amount of proteins but is also high in carbs)

- Shellfish – Lobster, mussels, clams, all good sources of protein, high in Omega 3's.

You can consume water-based drinks like coffees or tea while on the diet. They do not contain any carbohydrates and can help suppress appetite. In the morning to help kick start my day, I like to put a little heavy cream in my coffee and mix in a little MCT Oil. This helps to both satiate hunger and boost energy levels.

Spices

Spices are a great way to liven up your diet and can have great health benefits. A few of good spices include black pepper, basil, cayenne pepper, cilantro, cinnamon, cilantro, cumin, rosemary, sage, oregano, parsley, thyme, and turmeric. Some spices include have a small amount of carbs that you will need to be aware of. Be careful with hot sauces, as some have added sugar.

When cooking on a Ketogenic Diet, it is helpful to go beyond the recipes of this book and find alternatives to your favorite recipes. Since so much of our society's diet revolves around simple carbs, this section will give your for you ideas on how to inject healthy, low-carb/healthy alternatives that can be used in your tastiest dishes. Use alternate sources of flour instead of regular flour.

White wheat flour is a bad source of carbs and has little nutritional value, so try alternatives like coconut, almond, and other nut flours. Do you love baked potatoes, homemade fries, and wedges? You can replace the high-carb potato with baked root vegetables. Parsnips work wonderfully in recipes, and rutabaga/swede is a great replacement for potatoes. These vegetables have low carbs, high potassium, and taste great. Pasta and rice can be substituted by many vegetables. Use spaghetti squash in place of pasta. Fried zucchini in olive oil is a delicious and filling substitute for rice.

Shirataki noodles made from the konjac yam can also be used. They are gelatinous in texture but have a net carb count of zero. Shirataki noodles are filling, but they do not absorb flavor when used in soups and sauces. You might need to use strong seasonings with Shirataki noodles.

Try soybean noodles. They have up to 9.92 carbs per serving. You might find these noodles have a "different" texture, but they are awesome in soups and pasta dishes. Shredded cabbage also works well in place of pasta noodles. Fry up the cabbage and use it with your favorite meats and spices.

Use fresh and grated cauliflower as an alternative to rice, bulgur, and couscous. Cauliflower rice is very popular and is made by using a coarse grater. Boil the grated cauliflower and use in rice dishes.

Cheese and dairy can be high in fats, which is good for a Keto diet, but look out for those with added sugars. You would be surprised at how much sugar is added to milk; it's no wonder kids love it!

Foods to Avoid

You can eat very well on a Ketogenic Diet, but beware of some types of foods. Dieters have always heard that fruits are healthy a good on a diet, but not on a Ketogenic Diet. Fruits have natural sugars and having too much of them can take you out of ketosis. Raspberries, blueberries, and cranberries are delicious and are filled with antioxidants and phytonutrients; they can be enjoyed in moderate quantities. Here are a few foods you should avoid:

- **Hydrogenated fats** – These include margarine and some vegetable oils, as they are high in trans fats.

- **Beans** – Although they are high in fiber, they are also high in carbs, so it is best to eat sparingly.

- **Any pieces of bread** – Most bread contain little nutritional value, and they are very high in carbs.

- **Any pasta/rice** – Very high in carbs, even whole wheat pasta has little nutrients

- **Sugar** – Has no nutritional value and causes all sorts of health problems. Stay far away!

- **Tomato-based products** – Many are filled with added sugars. Make sure to read the nutrition labels to find out how much sugar and carbs these products contain!

- **Corn** – Very tasty but is one of the worst vegetables you can eat. It is a simple carbohydrate and converts to sugar almost immediately after it is digested!

- **Diets Sodas & Artificial Sweeteners** – Best to stay away from these while on a Ketogenic Diet; they may not have sugar that but can stop ketosis if you are not careful!

- **Alcohol** – Should be avoided because alcohol itself is a carbohydrate! But as with anything, moderation is key. Dry white wine is the best choice as it has the lowest sugar content of the wines. If you're a beer drinker, choose a low- carb beer like Michelob Ultra.

The Ketogenic Diet is an effective way to lose weight, but when you make dramatic changes to your diet, there can be mild side effects that you should be aware of as your body enters Ketosis.

1. **Do not forget your electrolytes: sodium, potassium, and magnesium** – As you change the way your body utilizes fats, you also need to adjust your electrolyte intake. Having adequate electrolyte levels can help you maintain equilibrium and fight off cravings. The electrolytes you need to focus on are sodium, potassium, and magnesium. Low sodium can cause dizziness and weakness. A great way to increase the sodium in your body is by drinking the home-made bone broth. If you lose sodium, chances are you'll lose potassium as well. Basil, Turmeric, Salmon, cocoa powder, tuna, and avocados are wonderful sources of potassium. Certain metabolic conditions on a Keto diet can cause insulin resistance which leads to magnesium excretion. You don't want this to happen. Add green leafy vegetables, mackerel, beans, and pumpkin seeds to ensure your body is getting the proper amount of magnesium.

2. **Learn to manage stress** – Stress not only causes mental turmoil but also physical symptoms. This can increase the cortisol level in your body, which in turn can increase your blood sugar level. This is a normal response to perceived threats and is useful in the fight or flight response. But, being in a constant state of stress can be detrimental. As it increases your blood sugar, it can decrease ketones and bring you out of the

ketosis state.

3. **Regular exercise** – Regular exercise causes your body to store carbohydrates in the muscles and liver. This means that you can tolerate more carbs without breaking out of ketosis. If you work out on a ketogenic diet, your body burns more fats; this is because you've already decreased the carbohydrates present in your body. This results in better muscle and strength development. A balanced workout routine should be combined with low-intensity and resistance training exercises.

4. **Hydrate, hydrate, hydrate!** – The Ketogenic Diet improves your body's ability to absorb insulin. This, in turn, causes increased urination and perspiration. If you don't replenish the lost fluids, you may become dehydrated. So you might need to drink more than you're used to as you become keto-adapted.

5. **Intermittent fasting** – Intermittent fasting means creating an eating schedule. It doesn't necessarily mean changing what you eat. You are only creating feeding and fasting schedules. This increases fat burning rates and metabolic adaptations. It limits your intake of calories as well. There are 3 approaches to fasting. The first involves skipping a meal a day; this usually is breakfast because it is the time of day when you are the least hungry. The second approach is creating fasting periods. This means not eating anything within a 12 to 16-hour time-frame. For example, you can eat breakfast at 7:00 AM and then nothing else until 7:00 PM. You can drink tea, coffee, and water during the fasting period. The last approach involves not eating anything solid for a full 24 hours; this may be difficult to do, but it can fast track weight

loss.

6. **Counter the loss of energy** – At the beginning of your Ketogenic Diet, you may experience headaches and a loss of energy. This is common when people first start out because your body is going through a sugar/glucose withdrawal, and just like an addict getting off of a drug, you may feel worse before you feel better! To help counter this, take multi-vitamins to help with fatigue, and use MCT Oil once a day to help with the grogginess.

7. **Add fiber** – Some people experience constipation when they begin a Ketogenic Diet. When you are on the diet, you may not get enough fiber that comes from eating carbohydrates. Be sure to eat enough green leafy vegetables to provide the fiber that you need. I find that a little MCT Oil also helps with this!

8. **Ease into it** – The best way to start is to ease your way into the Diet. First start off by making one meal fully Ketogenic. Then the next day doesn't drink any sweet drinks. After that make two meals that are Ketogenic so by the 4th or 5th day, your diet is fully Ketogenic. I find this helps to get people into the Diet that don't have much willpower (like myself), and you will slowly start to notice the diet work its magic, as you won't get hungry as much as you would on the first day.

At the end of the day, the biggest Shortcut to Ketosis lies in your ability to stay disciplined and balanced. So keep at it!

Chapter II

Keto Cereal

Star your day with this cereal! For more flavor, try toasting the coconut flakes ahead of time, or mix them together with stevia and cinnamon in a ziplock bag. During a busy day, all you need to do is put all of the ingredients together in a bowl. Instant cereal! You can also store this mix for later as a handy snack option.

Prep Time: 5 minutes; **Cook Time:** 5 minutes

Serving Size: 257 g; **Serves**: 1; **Calories:** 593

Total Fat: 121 g **Saturated Fat:** 17.8 g; **Trans Fat**: 0 g

Protein: 2.7 g; **Net Carbs:** 2.8 g

Total Carbs: 14 g; **Dietary Fibre:** 6.8 g; **Sugars:** 6.7 g

Cholesterol: 0 mg; **Sodium:** 13 mg; **Potassium**: 314 mg;

Vitamin A: 0%; **Vitamin C:** 65%; **Calcium**: 1%; **Iron:** 48%

Ingredients:

- ☐ *1 package of flaked coconut*
- ☐ *Ground cinnamon*
- ☐ *Stevia*
- ☐ *Almond milk*
- ☐ *A few medium sized strawberries*
- ☐ *Parchment paper and coconut oil*

Directions:

1. Preheat oven to 350 degrees.
2. Line a cookie sheet with parchment paper and cover with coconut oil.
3. Pour coconut flakes onto the cookie sheet.
4. Cook in the oven for five minutes.
5. Shuffle the flakes around and keep cooking until they are light brown and toasted.
6. Sprinkle lightly with cinnamon.
7. Pour ½ cup of the coconut chips into a bowl.
8. Pour the unsweetened almond milk over them.
9. Slice up strawberries for garnish and eat.

Coconut Pancakes

These high-fat pancakes are insanely delicious. They are pillowy, fluffy, super coconutty, tender, perfectly sweet, healthy, and easy to make. I love sprinkling the top with toasted coconut flake for a slightly crunchy version. You can even make these ahead of time, freeze them for up to 2 days, and then reheat them in the microwave.

Prep Time: 8 minutes; **Cook Time:** 6 minutes

Serving Size: 157 g; **Serves**: 1 (2 pieces 8-inch pancakes); **Calories:** 326

Total Fat: 26 g **Saturated Fat**: 14.3 g; **Trans Fat**: 0 g

Protein: 17.1g; **Net Carbs:** 1.6 g

Total Carbs: 2.5 g; **Dietary Fibre**: 0.9 g; **Sugars**: 1.7 g

Cholesterol: 522 mg; **Sodium**: 424 mg; **Potassium**: 216 mg;

Vitamin A: 0%; **Vitamin C**: 65%; **Calcium**: 1%; **Iron**: 48%

Ingredients:

- ☐ *3 eggs*

- ☐ *2 tablespoons coconut flour*
- ☐ *1 tablespoon butter*
- ☐ *Kosher salt*

Directions:

1. In mixing bowl, beat the eggs, coconut flour, a pinch of salt until well combined.

2. In a non-stick skillet over medium heat, melt 1/2 tablespoon of the butter.

3. Pour half of the batter mixture. Cook for about 2, flip, and then cook for about 1 minute more or until the pancake is cooked through. Cook the remaining batter with the remaining 1/2 tablespoon butter. Serve topped with leftover meat or avocado slices, if desired.

French Toast Pancake

I wanted something more flavorful than the simple 2-ingredient recipe cream cheese pancake. I experimented in the kitchen, and this is what I came up with – a low-carb, gluten-free pancake that tastes quite a bit like French toast! Hence, the name!

Prep Time: 5 minutes; **Cook Time:** 8 minutes

Serving Size: 164 g; **Serves:** 1; **Calories:** 397

Total Fat: 9.3 g **Saturated Fat:** 19.4 g; **Trans Fat:** 0 g

Protein: 15.9 g; **Net Carbs:** 7.4 g

Total Carbs: 9.3 g; **Dietary Fibre:** 1.9 g; **Sugars:** 5.7 g

Cholesterol: 390 mg; **Sodium:** 294 mg; **Potassium:** 241 mg;

Vitamin A: 24%; **Vitamin C:** 1%; **Calcium:** 10%; **Iron:** 24%

Ingredients:

- ☐ *2 eggs*
- ☐ *2 ounces cream cheese*
- ☐ *1 tablespoons coconut flour*
- ☐ *1/2 teaspoon cinnamon*
- ☐ *1/2–1 packet Stevia*
- ☐ *Sugar-free maple syrup or butter*
- ☐ *Salted butter or coconut oil*

Directions:

1. Put all of the ingredients in a blender. Blend until smooth.

2. In a non-stick skillet or pan, heat the salted butter

29

over medium high.

3. Pour 1/2 of the batter into the skillet. Cook for 2 minutes, flip, and cook for 1 minute more on until the pancake is cooked. Top with butter or maple syrup.

Spicy Keto Omelet

This healthy and quick breakfast idea came to me when I had leftover shrimp from the night before. They looked lonely sitting on their own, so I thought they'd love a little bit of company. I gathered up what I had in the pantry and the fridge, and came up with this very pleasing omelet. I love spicy food, so I made my version hotter with more cayenne.

Prep Time: 10 minutes; **Cook Time:** 5 minutes

Serving Size: 239 g; **Serves**: 4; **Calories**: 248
Total Fat: 20.6 g **Saturated Fat**: 16.8 g; **Trans Fat**: 0 g
Protein: 10.2 g; **Net Carbs**: 5.7 g
Total Carbs: 8.1 g; **Dietary Fibre**: 2.4 g; **Sugars**: 4.6 g
Cholesterol: 81 mg; **Sodium**: 96 mg; **Potassium**: 515 mg;
Vitamin A: 50%; **Vitamin C**: 38%; **Calcium**: 5%; **Iron**: 6%

Ingredients:

- ☐ *10 large shrimps*
- ☐ *30 ml of almond milk*
- ☐ *Six eggs (4-5 are egg whites, and 1 is the egg yolk)*
- ☐ *4 grape tomatoes*
- ☐ *5 tablespoons coconut oil*
- ☐ *1/8 pound of spinach*
- ☐ *1 small onion*
- ☐ *1 sprig of parsley*
- ☐ *¼ teaspoon of cayenne pepper*

Directions:

1. Chop the veggies.

2. Beat the egg whites, egg yolk, and almond milk together.

3. Coat a small frying pan with coconut oil.

4. Sauté the veggies until they are soft.

5. Remove the veggies and pour in the eggs.

6. When the eggs are firm, place ½ the veggies on ½ the egg mixtures.

7. Fold the egg mixture over the top.

8. Place the remaining veggies on the top of the omelet.

9. Eat and enjoy!

Good Morning Salad

Salad for breakfast? Why not? Salad mixed with carrots, aged vinegar, and warm runny eggs on top is a great wake-up meal to start the day. Leftover grilled steak is a perfect addition to this salad.

Prep Time: 5 minutes; **Cook Time**: 10 minutes	
Serving Size: 336 g; **Serves**: 1; **Calories**: 421	
Total Fat: 34.1 g **Saturated Fat**: 18.6 g; **Trans Fat**: 0 g	
Protein: 15.2 g; **Net Carbs**: 10.7 g	
Total Carbs: 16 g; **Dietary Fibre**: 5.3 g; **Sugars**: 4.2 g	
Cholesterol: 393 mg; **Sodium**: 454 mg; **Potassium**: 351 mg;	
Vitamin A: 312%; **Vitamin C**: 19%; **Calcium**: 12%; **Iron**: 15%	

Ingredients:

- ☐ *2 eggs, large*
- ☐ *2 cups salad greens mix*
- ☐ *1 large carrot, peeled*
- ☐ *2 tablespoon ghee, heaping*
- ☐ *Sea salt, flake*
- ☐ *Black pepper, freshly ground*
- ☐ *Balsamic vinegar or sherry vinegar, aged*

Directions:

1. Heat a small cast-iron skillet on high until very hot.

2. In the meantime, pile the salad greens into a salad bowl.

3. Shred or vegetable peel the carrots over the lettuce.

4. When the skillet it very hot, pour the ghee.

5. Crack two eggs into a bowl and then pour them into the skillet.

6. Tilt the skillet away from you to avoid the spitting oil from splattering on you. With an offset spoon, baste the egg whites near the yolk with the ghee. When the egg whites near the yolks are cooked through, and the bottom is golden brown and crispy, turn the heat off.

7. With a fish spatula, remove the eggs and top them with the salad, drizzling any excess ghee over the salad; season with the salt and pepper to taste and drizzle with balsamic vinegar.

Creamy Cheesy Asparagus Frittata

This is combining everything you love in a skillet and then baking them into flavorful, cheesy, fluffy perfection. This breakfast-dinner dish or briner is both delicious and easy to make. Not only does this taste great, but your house will also smell amazing when the frittata is cooked.

Prep Time: 15 minutes; **Cook Time:** 30 minutes

Serving Size: 159 g; **Serves:** 8; **Calories:** 258

Total Fat: 20.4 g **Saturated Fat:** 9.6 g; **Trans Fat:** 0 g

Protein: 13 g; **Net Carbs:** 3.2 g

Total Carbs: 4.5 g; **Dietary Fibre:** 1.3 g; **Sugars:** 1.9 g

Cholesterol: 222 mg; **Sodium:** 334 mg; **Potassium:** 218 mg;

Vitamin A: 21%; **Vitamin C:** 6%; **Calcium:** 20%; **Iron:** 13%

Ingredients:

☐ *8 large eggs*

- [ ] *1-pound asparagus, choose slender stalks if available, ends trimmed*
- [ ] *1/2 cup Parmesan cheese, grated, divided*
- [ ] *1 cup Swiss cheese, shredded*
- [ ] *4 tablespoons butter*
- [ ] *1/4 cup heavy cream*
- [ ] *1/2 teaspoon salt*
- [ ] *1/2 teaspoon dried thyme*
- [ ] *1/2 small onion*
- [ ] *1/2 cup dry white wine*
- [ ] *2 tablespoons-worth nonstick cooking spray, for greasing*

Directions:

1. Lay the asparagus stalks on a cutting board. Cut each stalk into 1/2 inches.

2. Grease a heavy oven-safe skillet well with cooking spray. Place over medium-low heat. Melt the butter. Put the onion. Sauté until soft and translucent.

3. Add the asparagus. Sauté for 1–2 minutes or until the stalks turn brighter green.

4. In a mixing bowl, whisk the remaining ingredients together. Pour into the skillet. Stir around until the onions and the asparagus are distributed evenly.

5. Adjust the heat to low. Cover the skillet. Cook for about 15–20 minutes. Check. If the frittata is still runny, cook for additional 5–10 minutes.

6. When the frittata is just a little runny, transfer the

skillet to the oven about 6 inches from the heat. Broil for until the top is just golden. Cut into wedges. Serve.

D.I.Y. Ghee or Clarified Butter

This is a must staple for your low-carb lifestyle, especially for those who have a problem with casein or lactose. Cooking butter removes not only the water but the sugars and the milk proteins as well. Ghee is ideal for roasting, sautéing, stir-frying, and all your other dishes that need to be cooked on high heat.

Prep Time: 1-2 minutes; **Cook Time:** 15 minutes

Serving Size: 14 g ; **Makes:** 3/4 cup (about 16 tablespoons); **Calories:** 102

Total Fat: 11.5 g **Saturated Fat:** 7.3 g; **Trans Fat:** 0 g

Protein: 0.1 g; **Net Carbs:** 0 g

Total Carbs: 0 g; **Dietary Fibre:** 0 g; **Sugars:** 0 g

Cholesterol: 31 mg; **Sodium:** 82 mg; **Potassium:** 3 mg;

Vitamin A: 7%; **Vitamin C:** 0%; **Calcium:** 0%; **Iron:** 0%

Ingredients:

☐ *1 cup (2 sticks) unsalted butter*

Directions:

1. In a saucepan, melt the butter over low heat. As the butter melts, the milk solids and the clear fat will separate.

2. Continue simmering gently, keeping a close watch. Bubbles will form and will these will get smaller until the surface of the melted butter resembles foam. You will begin to see the milk solids turning brown and clumping together.

3. About 8–10 minutes after the butter starts bubbling,

the milk solids will turn golden brown and will start falling to the bottom of the saucepan. Remove the pan from the heat.

4. Place a fine-mesh strainer over a heat-safe cup or bowl. Tuck a triple layer cheesecloth into the strainer. Carefully pour and strain the butter through the cheesecloth. Discard the milk solids.

5. Store the ghee in a sealed container. There is no need to store the ghee in the refrigerator, but if you decide to keep it in the fridge, it will last up to a year.

Feta Cheese and Pesto Sauce Omelet with Grilled Vegetable

This is a great way to give leftover vegetables a new look and a different taste. What I like to do is place the omelet in a deep plate, top it with the heated grilled vegetables, drizzle pesto sauce all over the veggies, and then sprinkle it with the cheese and sea salt. It's a new dish that barely resembles what you ate just last night!

Prep Time: 10 minutes; **Cook Time:** 10 minutes

Serving Size: 143 g ; **Serves:** 1; **Calories:** 406

Total Fat: 37.8 g **Saturated Fat**: 8.6 g; **Trans Fat**: 0 g

Protein: 15.4 g; **Net Carbs:** 2.6 g

Total Carbs: 3.1 g; **Dietary Fibre:** 0.5 g; **Sugars:** 0 g

Cholesterol: 343 mg; **Sodium:** 418 mg; **Potassium:** 124 mg;

Vitamin A: 1%; **Vitamin C:** 0%; **Calcium:** 19%; **Iron**: 10%

Ingredients:

- ☐ *1 tablespoon olive oil or butter*
- ☐ *2 eggs, well beaten*
- ☐ *2 tablespoons pesto sauce*
- ☐ *1 tablespoon feta cheese*
- ☐ *Optional: 1 1/2 cups leftover grilled vegetables, chopped*
- ☐ *For taste: Sea salt*

Directions:

1. If using vegetables, pour vegetables in a small pot, cover, and heat over medium-low heat. When sufficiently heated, set aside.
2. Over medium heat, heat the oil in a small skillet.
3. In a bowl, whisk the eggs until well beaten.
4. Pour the beaten eggs into the skillet. Cook for about 2–3 minutes or until the center and sides of the eggs are firm. Carefully flip. Cook for an additional 10–20 seconds.
5. When cooked, transfer to a plate. Stuff the vegetables.
6. Serve with feta cheese, pesto sauce, and a sprinkle of sea salt.

Keto Mexican Guacamole

This is a Keto version of a famous Mexican recipe is a high-fat dip that is perfect for your low-carb life. This dip mainly made up of avocado, which is made up of 75% fat, predominantly of monounsaturated fat, and is great to use as a regular topping or spread. Avocado, is also packed with B vitamins, vitamins K and E, potassium, and high in fiber, making it an excellent Shortcut to Ketosis.

Prep Time: 5 minutes; **Cook Time:** 15 minutes

Serving Size: 153 g; **Serves:** 4; **Calories:** 309

Total Fat: 29.4 g **Saturated Fat:** 6.2 g; **Trans Fat:** 0 g

Protein: 2.9 g; **Net Carbs:** 3.3 g

Total Carbs: 13.4 g; **Dietary Fibre:** 10.1 g; **Sugars:** 0.8 g

Cholesterol: 0 mg; **Sodium:** 48 mg; **Potassium:** 740 mg;

Vitamin A: 5%; **Vitamin C:** 25%; **Calcium:** 2%; **Iron:** 5%

Ingredients:

- ☐ *1 lime, juice*
- ☐ *1 small shallot; mince*
- ☐ *3 avocados*
- ☐ *Chili powder or Aleppo pepper (optional)*
- ☐ *Freshly ground pepper*
- ☐ *Kosher salt, about 3 generous pinches*

Directions:

1. Mix the minced shallot, lime juice and salt in a medium-sized bowl. Allow to sit for 10 minutes.

2. Cut the avocado in half, pit, and peel. Place in a bowl, one-half of the avocado slices and mash using a fork.

3. Pour the lime mixture into the bowl of mashed avocado. Combine.

4. Dice the remaining avocado into 3/4 inch cubes. Gently mix in the bowl of mashed avocado.

5. Add ground pepper and chili pepper to taste, if desired.

Breakfast Green Eggs

Sam-I-Am would certainly love this version of green eggs. It's a journey of a whimsically delicious breakfast in the world of Dr. Seuss. Top this dish with a spoonful or two of Keto Mexican Guacamole and low-carb salsa, and your tastes buds will thank you.

Prep Time: 5 minutes; **Cook Time:** 15 minutes

Serving Size: 187 g; **Serves:** 1; **Calories:** 351

Total Fat: 32 g **Saturated Fat**: 17.4 g; **Trans Fat:** 0 g

Protein: 13.3 g; **Net Carbs:** 3.2 g

Total Carbs: 4.6 g; **Dietary Fibre:** 1.4 g; **Sugars:** 0 g

Cholesterol: 388 mg; **Sodium**: 490 mg; **Potassium**: 494 mg;

Vitamin A: 138%; **Vitamin C**: 29%; **Calcium**: 12%; **Iron**: 19%

Ingredients:

☐ *2 eggs*

- [ ] *2 cups frozen spinach*
- [ ] *1 small shallot*
- [ ] *2 tablespoons butter*
- [ ] *Salt*
- [ ] *Black pepper*

Directions:

1. Heat up the spinach in the microwave for about 1 minute to defrost.

2. While the spinach is heating up, mince shallot. In a small cast iron skillet over medium heat, heat the butter. Put the shallot in and sauté.

3. Beat the eggs with the salt and pepper. Squeeze out the liquid from the spinach. Add into the egg mix. Stir to combine. Pour into the skillet, making sure the shallots are distributed. Lower the heat to medium-low. Cook until the frittata is set, flip, and continue cooking until thoroughly cooked. Serve with guacamole and salsa, if desired.

Liverwurst Omelet

There is a reason why you should incorporate liver into your breakfast egg meals. It packs your low-carb breakfast with not just the fat you need, but also with a whopping 313% of vitamin A and 30% of vitamin C as well. This omelet is also very high in vitamin B12, B3, B5, the antioxidant selenium, and a good source of other vitamins and minerals.

Prep Time: 10 minutes; **Cook Time:** 10 minutes

Serving Size: 275 g; **Serves:** 1; **Calories:** 613

Total Fat: 49 g **Saturated Fat:** 17.9 g; **Trans Fat:** 0 g

Protein: 32.8 g; **Net Carbs:** 9.4 g

Total Carbs: 10.1 g; **Dietary Fibre:** 0.7 g; **Sugars:** 3.3 g

Cholesterol: 629 mg; **Sodium:** 466 mg; **Potassium:** 480 mg;

Vitamin A: 318%; **Vitamin C**: 15%; **Calcium**: 19%; **Iron**: 31%

Ingredients:

- ☐ *2 ounces liverwurst, sliced*
- ☐ *2 large eggs*
- ☐ *1/2 medium tomato, sliced*
- ☐ *1 tablespoon Parmesan cheese, grated*
- ☐ *1 tablespoon mayonnaise*
- ☐ *2 tablespoon bacon grease or butter*

Directions:

1. Whisk the eggs. Heat the bacon grease or butter in a skillet over medium heat. Cook until the omelet

is almost done.

2. Put the liverwurst over the omelet. Top with the tomato. Fold the omelet and continue cooking until thoroughly cooked.

3. Top with the mayonnaise and the cheese. Serve.

Breakfast Salsa

This recipe is a family dish. It's a delicious breakfast made with bacon and tomatoes. Serve with eggs.

Prep Time: 5 minutes; **Cook Time:** 10 minutes	
Serving Size: 58 g; **Serves:** 6; **Calories:** 119	
Total Fat: 10.4 g **Saturated Fat:** 5.3 g; **Trans Fat:** 0 g	
Protein: 4.0 g; **Net Carbs:** 1.9 g	
Total Carbs: 2.6 g; **Dietary Fibre:** 0.7 g; **Sugars:** 1.6 g	
Cholesterol: 27 mg; **Sodium:** 327 mg; **Potassium:** 164 mg;	
Vitamin A: 8%; **Vitamin C:** 8%; **Calcium:** 1%; **Iron:** 2%	

Ingredients:

- ☐ 9 slices bacon
- ☐ 1/2 onion, chopped
- ☐ 1 fresh jalapeno pepper, seeded, chopped
- ☐ 1 fresh tomato, finely chopped
- ☐ 1/2 cup tomato sauce, canned
- ☐ 3 tablespoons ghee

Directions:

1. Place the bacon slices in a deep, large-sized skillet; cook until evenly browned over medium-high heat.

2. Remove from the pan; transfer to a plate. Add the ghee in the pan. Add the onions, tomato, and pepper;

sauté for about 3 minutes or until the onion is soft.

3. Crumble the bacon into the pan. Stir in the tomato sauce; continue cooking until the mixture is heated through.

Baked Eggs and Avocado

Baking eggs and avocado together is a great way of filling your day with the heart-healthy fat omega 3. The baked eggs and bacon come out warm and creamy. Topped with delicious crispy salty bacon crumbs, this makes for a scrumptious morning meal!

Prep Time: 10 minutes; **Cook Time:** 15 minutes

Serving Size: 157 g; **Serves:** 2; **Calories:** 361

Total Fat: 31.2 g **Saturated Fat:** 7.9 g; **Trans Fat:** 0 g

Protein: 13.6 g; **Net Carbs:** 5.9 g

Total Carbs: 6.7 g; **Dietary Fibre:** 0.8 g; **Sugars:** 0.8 g

Cholesterol: 159 mg; **Sodium:** 497 mg; **Potassium:** 644 mg;

Vitamin A: 7%; **Vitamin C:** 17%; **Calcium:** 3%; **Iron:** 9%

Ingredients

- ☐ *1 avocado; cut in half and pit*

- ☐ *2 slices bacon, cooked and crumbled*
- ☐ *2 small eggs*

To season:

- ☐ *Chives*
- ☐ *Parsley*
- ☐ *Sea salt*
- ☐ *Pepper*

Directions:

1. Preheat oven to 425F (220C).

2. Carefully crack the eggs into a bowl, making sure the yolks remain intact.

3. Arrange the avocado halves in a baking dish. Rest them along the edge so they will not tip over. Gently and carefully, spoon 1 egg yolk into an avocado pit. Spoon egg white into the avocado until the pit is full. Repeat the process for the other avocado half.

4. Season each filled the avocado pit with parsley, chives, salt, and pepper.

5. Carefully place the baking dish in the oven; bake for about 15 minutes or until the eggs are cooked. Sprinkle crumbled bacon over the cooked avocado and eggs.

Breakfast Ham Cups

These bite sized bites are perfect for a weekend breakfast. They are crunchy and salty on the outside while cheesy, and fluffy on the inside. They can be enjoyed on the go as well and be eaten straight out of the fridge cold. Can also be even enjoyed as snacks or served as appetizers.

Prep Time: 10 minutes; **Cook Time:** 15 minutes	
Serving Size: 188 g; **Serves:** 6; **Calories:** 360	
Total Fat: 30.1 g **Saturated Fat:** 8.5 g; **Trans Fat:** 0 g	
Protein: 15.2 g; **Net Carbs:** 3.1 g	
Total Carbs: 10.2 g; **Dietary Fibre:** 7.1 g; **Sugars:** 0.9 g	
Cholesterol: 212 mg; **Sodium:** 539 mg; **Potassium:** 644 mg;	
Vitamin A: 10%; **Vitamin C:** 19%; **Calcium:** 11%; **Iron:** 10%	

Ingredients:

- ☐ *6 slices ham*
- ☐ *6 large eggs*
- ☐ *1/2 cup cheddar cheese, grated*
- ☐ *Black pepper, freshly ground or cayenne pepper*
- ☐ *Pinch sea salt or Himalayan salt*

Optional:

- ☐ *3 medium avocados, diced*

Directions:

1. Preheat the oven to 350F or 175C.

2. Into the cups of a muffin tin, place a slice of ham, creating small cones. Put cheese into each cup. Reserve any remaining cheese for topping.

3. Crack an egg into each cup; season with the salt and pepper.

4. Top with the remaining cheese or diced avocado. Place the muffin tin into the oven. Cook for about 15 minutes.

Radish Scramble

Radishes are great substitutes for potatoes. Not only are they low carb, but they also cook almost exactly like potatoes. Scrambled with the eggs, pancetta, and flank steak makes this meal a delicious high-fat, high protein breakfast that is packed with Vitamins A and C, calcium, and iron.

Prep Time: 20 minutes; **Cook Time:** 10 minutes

Serving Size: 399 g; **Serves:** 2; **Calories:** 982

Total Fat: 76.1 g **Saturated Fat**: 26.6 g; **Trans Fat**: 0 g

Protein: 67.8 g; **Net Carbs:** 3.3 g

Total Carbs: 4.7 g; **Dietary Fibre:** 1.4 g; **Sugars:** 2.6 g

Cholesterol: 480 mg; **Sodium**: 1227 mg; **Potassium**: 916 mg;

Vitamin A: 20%; **Vitamin C**: 50%; **Calcium**: 21%; **Iron**: 27%

Ingredients

- ☐ *8 ounce. flank steak*
- ☐ *6 ounce. Radishes*
- ☐ *2 ounce cubetti pancetta*
- ☐ *4 ounce. cheddar cheese*
- ☐ *4 eggs*
- ☐ *4 tablespoons cooking oil*
- ☐ *Salt and pepper to taste*

Directions

1. Preheat oven to 450 degrees.
2. Add the cooking oil; heat.

3. Add the flank steak, pan-fry for 3 minutes. Remove from the pan, set aside, and let cool.

4. Meanwhile, wash the radishes, and cut off the ends. Quarter the radishes.

5. Pan-fry the radishes and pancetta in a cast iron skillet for about 6 minutes or until the radishes turn golden brown.

6. Slice the flank steak and add into the pan.

7. Add the cheese.

8. Break the eggs into the mixture, season to taste and cook for a minute to set the bottom of the pan.

9. Transfer to the oven and cook for 8 minutes, boiling for an additional 4 minutes or until the eggs are set.

Eggs Benedict Sandwich

Missing bread? Then make your cream cheese Oopsie rolls (see recipe below). These no carb and no flour rolls are good substitutes for real bread and are easy to whip up. Topped with Canadian bacon, poached egg, and hollandaise sauce, this sandwich is a perfect breakfast. This version is a high fat, high-protein, rich in vitamins and minerals meal that is exactly what you need to start the day right.

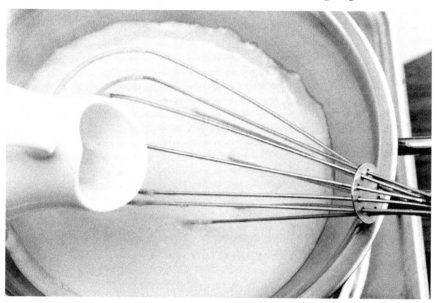

Prep Time: 10 minutes; **Cook Time:** 10 minutes

Serving Size: 153 g; **Serves:** 4; **Calories:** 316

Total Fat: 25.7 g **Saturated Fat**: 12.3 g; **Trans Fat**: 0 g

Protein: 19.2 g; **Net Carbs:** 2.2 g

Total Carbs: 2.2 g; **Dietary Fibre:** 0 g; **Sugars:** 0.8 g

Cholesterol: 461 mg; **Sodium:** 737 mg; **Potassium**: 267 mg;

Vitamin A: 21%; **Vitamin C:** 1%; **Calcium:** 8%; **Iron**: 12%

Ingredients:

- [ ] *4 eggs*
- [ ] *1 tablespoon vinegar*
- [ ] *1 tsp. chives*
- [ ] *4 Oopsie rolls*
- [ ] *4 slices Canadian back bacon*

Hollandaise Sauce:

- [ ] *2 egg yolks*
- [ ] *2 tablespoons butter*
- [ ] *2 pinch paprika*
- [ ] *1 tsp lemon juice*
- [ ] *a pinch of salt*

Directions:

1. Make a quick hollandaise sauce.

2. Separate 2 eggs and whisk the yolks in a glass bowl until they've doubled in volume.

3. Add a splash of lemon juice.

4. Boil a pot of water and melt butter. Add to the sauce to emulsify.

5. Use a double boiler and whisk the egg yolks rapidly. They become thicker the more your whisk but do not cook the too much or they will become scrambled eggs. Hollandaise Sauce should be spoonable.

6. Poach your eggs in a pot of water. Use about 3 inches of water.

7. Once the water comes to a boil, reduce it to a simmer

and add salt and white vinegar.

8. Create a whirlpool in the water with a wooden spoon – stir the water around a few times in one direction.

9. Crack an egg into a teacup and gently lower it into the whirlpool you have created. Lower the egg into the water; don't drop the egg in.

10. Cook the egg for about 2-4 minutes. The eggs need to be runny.

11. Live the egg out with a spatula and rest it on a paper towel.

12. Fry up the Canadian bacon.

13. Top 4 Oopsie rolls with the Canadian bacon and places poached egg on top

14. Spoon hollandaise sauce onto each poached egg, add salt and pepper, and enjoy!

Ham, Egg, Spinach, and Coconut Pancakes

If you loved coconut pancakes, then you will love this ham and spinach stuffed version. These egg patties are savory and truly yummy!

Prep Time: 15 minutes; **Cook Time:** 15 minutes	
Serving Size: 72 g (1 pancake); **Serves:** 3 (2 pancakes each); **Calories:** 214	
Total Fat: 20.2 g **Saturated Fat:** 13.4 g; **Trans Fat:** 0 g	
Protein: 7.7 g; **Net Carbs:** 1.1 g	
Total Carbs: 1.9 g; **Dietary Fibre:** 0.8 g; **Sugars:** 0 g	
Cholesterol: 133 mg; **Sodium:** 377 mg; **Potassium:** 147 mg;	
Vitamin A:13%; **Vitamin C:** 4%; **Calcium:** 4%; **Iron:** 6%	

Ingredients:

- ☐ 1 cup frozen spinach; thaw and squeeze dry (about 1/3 cup squeezed dried spinach)
- ☐ 1 tablespoon fresh chives, minced or Sunny Paris seasoning
- ☐ 1/2 teaspoon baking soda
- ☐ 1/2 teaspoon apple cider vinegar
- ☐ 1/4 cup coconut flour
- ☐ 2/3 cup ham, diced (or any available leftover cooked meat)
- ☐ 4 large eggs
- ☐ Freshly ground black pepper
- ☐ For frying: 6 tablespoons coconut oil or ghee
- ☐ To taste: Kosher salt

Directions:

1. Whisk together the eggs, minced fresh chives or Sunny Paris seasoning, and salt (to taste) large bowl. Stir in the coconut flour and the baking soda into the egg mix. Add the ham, spinach, vinegar into the egg-flour batter. Stir everything to combine.

2. In a cast iron skillet, heat 1 tablespoon of coconut oil or ghee over medium heat. Pour or scoop about 3 tablespoons of the batter into the skillet.

3. Spread the batter to about 1/2 inch using the back of a spoon.

4. Cook for about 2 minutes, flip and cook the other side for 1 minute.

5. Transfer cooked the pancake on a wire rack to cool. Cook the rest of the batter. Serve plain or topped with breakfast salsa or keto Mexican guacamole.

Bacon and Egg Cheese Baskets

These baskets are deliciously crispy. Frying eggs in bacon fat gives the dish rich, deep flavor. Topped with low-carb salsa, this will burst out with cool, fresh sweet taste that complements the cheese, eggs, and bacon.

Prep Time: 15 minutes; **Cook Time:** 15 minutes	
Serving Size: 111 g (1 basket); **Serves:** 3 (2 baskets each); **Calories:** 306	
Total Fat: 26.1 g **Saturated Fat:** 9.7 g; **Trans Fat:** 0 g	
Protein: 16 g; **Net Carbs:** 1.1 g	
Total Carbs: 2.3 g; **Dietary Fibre:** 0.5 g; **Sugars:** 1.1 g	
Cholesterol: 223 mg; **Sodium:** 682 mg; **Potassium:** 192 mg;	
Vitamin A: 16%; **Vitamin C:** 1%; **Calcium:** 24%; **Iron:** 8%	

Ingredients:

- ☐ *1 1/2 cup cheese*
- ☐ *6 tablespoons salsa*
- ☐ *6 slices bacon*
- ☐ *6 large eggs*
- ☐ *4 tablespoons cooking oil*
- ☐ *1/4 teaspoon cayenne pepper*
- ☐ *1/2 teaspoon salt*
- ☐ *1 teaspoon pepper*
- ☐ *1 teaspoon paprika*

Directions:

1. Line your baking sheet with Silpat mat or parchment

paper. Form 6 circular piles (about 3–4 inches in diameter) of cheese; season with paprika and cayenne pepper. Bake at 400F for about 10–12 minutes. Immediately after baking, mold 3 of them on an upside down cupcake tray, leaving the 3 baskets flat. Set aside.

2. Cut the bacon into thin slices. Cook in a non-stick pan until very crisp with the cooking oil. Transfer to a paper towel lined plate, keeping as much bacon grease as possible in the pan.

3. In the same pan, fry the 3 eggs separately. Using a cookie cutter, cut the egg whites edges to create a circular egg. Scramble the remaining 3 eggs in the skillet; season with salt and pepper.

4. Top the circular friend eggs on the flat cheese baskets. Top the scrambled eggs on the molded baskets. Top each with the bacon and 1 tablespoon salsa. Serve.

Keto Lemon-Poppy Seed Muffins

These muffins are fast and easy to make. They are also great to store and are freezable as well. Perfect when you are in a hurry during a busy weekday. Heat a piece in the microwave for about 15-20 seconds, slice in half, and dab a slice of butter between the slices for extra fat. You can also enjoy them as a snack topped with whipped cream cheese frosting.

Prep Time: 15 minutes; **Cook Time:** 20 minutes	
Serving Size: 44 g; **Serves:** 12; **Calories:** 120	
Total Fat: 10.4 g **Saturated Fat:** 3.8 g; **Trans Fat:** 0 g	
Protein: 3.8 g; **Net Carbs:** 1.1 g	
Total Carbs: 3.7 g; **Dietary Fibre:** 1.8 g; **Sugars:** 0.9 g	
Cholesterol: 60 mg; **Sodium:** 48 mg; **Potassium:** 154 mg;	
Vitamin A: 4%; **Vitamin C:** 12%; **Calcium:** 7%; **Iron:** 8%	

Ingredients:

- [ ] *3/4 cup almond flour*
- [ ] *1/4 cup flaxseed meal*
- [ ] *1/3 cup Erythritol*
- [ ] *1 teaspoon baking powder*
- [ ] *2 tablespoon poppy seeds*
- [ ] *1/4 cup melted butter*
- [ ] *1/4 cup heavy cream*
- [ ] *3 large eggs*
- [ ] *Zest of 2 lemons*
- [ ] *3 tablespoons lemon juice*
- [ ] *1 teaspoon vanilla extract*

Directions:

1. Preheat oven to 350F.

2. Combine almond flour, flaxseed meal, Erythritol and poppy seeds.

3. Stir in melted butter, eggs, and heavy cream. Mix until no lumps are in the batter.

4. Add in baking powder, vanilla extract, lemon zest, and lemon juice. Mix thoroughly.

5. Pour batter into baking cups.

6. Bake for 18-20 minutes or until slightly browned.

7. Remove from the oven and cool for about 10 minutes.

8. Makes a total of 12 Keto Lemon Poppy Seed Muffins

BLT Avocado

These bacon, lettuce, and tomato stuffed avocado halves are gluten-free and paleo-friendly. They can be enjoyed as a snack or a lunch meal. You can pack them in a cooler for a picnic or in your lunch bag to bring to work the next day. Skip the boring bread of the usual BLT sandwich with this low carb version.

Prep Time: 10 minutes; **Cook Time:** 5 minutes

Serving Size: 135 g; **Serves:** 4 (1/2 avocado each); **Calories:** 228

Total Fat: 21 g Saturated Fat: 4.6 g; **Trans Fat:** 0 g

Protein: 3.3 g; **Net Carbs:** 3 g

Total Carbs: 10.1 g; **Dietary Fibre:** 7.1 g; **Sugars:** 1.2 g

Cholesterol: 3 mg; **Sodium:** 198 mg; **Potassium:** 573 mg;

Vitamin A: 7%; **Vitamin C:** 23%; **Calcium:** 2%; **Iron:** 5%

Ingredients:

- ☐ 2 slices bacon
- ☐ 2 medium avocados
- ☐ 1/8 tsp black pepper
- ☐ 1/4 tsp sea salt
- ☐ 1/4 tsp garlic powder
- ☐ 1/2 cup romaine lettuce, chopped
- ☐ 1/2 cup grape tomatoes, halved
- ☐ 1 tsp lime juice

Directions:

1. While the skillet is still cold, place the bacon in. Turn on flame/heat to low or medium-low; cook the bacon until the edges begin to curl. Flip the slices; continue cooking until crispy and golden. Transfer to a plate and let cool.

2. Meanwhile, slice the avocado into halves and remove the pits. Scoop half of the flesh out of the avocado halves with disturbing the remaining half; transfer the scooped out flesh into a bowl.

3. Mash the avocado flesh in the bowl. Stir in the lettuce, tomatoes, lime juice, sea salt, garlic powder, and pepper. Taste and adjust seasoning, if needed.

4. Chop the bacon; add to the bowl. Stir to mix.

5. Scoop the mixture back into the avocado halves.

Almond Butter Pancakes

These pancakes are grain-free. This breakfast closely resembles a stack of real pancakes, both in flavor and texture. Most will not believe they are flour-less. For added flavor, top with sugar-free maple syrup.

Prep Time: 5 minutes; **Cook Time:** 30 minutes	
Serving Size: 115 g; **Serves:** 4; **Calories:** 496	
Total Fat: 46.6 g **Saturated Fat**: 17.2 g; **Trans Fat**: 0 g	
Protein: 14.8 g; **Net Carbs:** 3 g	
Total Carbs: 9.7 g; **Dietary Fibre:** 1.8 g; **Sugars:** 0 g	
Cholesterol: 150 mg; **Sodium:** 131 mg; **Potassium:** 601 mg;	
Vitamin A: 6%; **Vitamin C:** 1%; **Calcium**: 23%; **Iron**: 14%	

Ingredients:

- [ ] *3/4 cup almond butter*
- [ ] *3 large eggs*
- [ ] *2 tablespoons water*
- [ ] *1/8 teaspoon salt*

- *1/4 cup heavy cream*
- *1/4 cup coconut oil*
- *1 1/2 teaspoons baking powder*

Directions:

1. Over medium heat, heat a heavy, large nonstick skillet or a girdle.

2. Put all of the ingredients into a blender. Blend until you have a smooth batter.

3. Grease the skillet or girdle with 1 tablespoon coconut oil. Pour batter into the skillet or girdle. Cook until the bottom side is browned. Flip and continue cooking until thoroughly cooked.

Meat Loaf Muffins

These bite-sized breakfast meals are nutritious and flavorful. This dish is very high in protein and is loaded with iron. Meal Prep tip: You can make the muffins ahead time, individually wrap them up, and throw them in them in the freezer. You can later use them anytime you a need a quick breakfast or snack.

Prep Time: 10 minutes; **Cook Time:** 30 minutes

Serving Size: 115 (1 muffin) g; **Serves:** 4-6; **Calories:** 496

Total Fat: 18.3 g **Saturated Fat:** 3.2 g; **Trans Fat:** 0 g

Protein: 12.8 g; **Net Carbs:** 2.5 g

Total Carbs: 3.3 g; **Dietary Fibre:** 0.8 g; **Sugars:** 1.6 g

Cholesterol: 49 mg; **Sodium:** 48 mg; **Potassium:** 269 mg;

Vitamin A: 12%; **Vitamin C:** 12%; **Calcium:** 2%; **Iron:** 43%

Ingredients:

- ☐ *1 1/2 pounds beef, ground*
- ☐ *1/2 cup button mushrooms, finely diced*
- ☐ *1 large egg*
- ☐ *1 tablespoon ground mustard*
- ☐ *1 teaspoon dried thyme*
- ☐ *1 teaspoon fresh rosemary, finely minced*
- ☐ *1/2 cup green bell pepper, finely chopped*
- ☐ *1/2 teaspoon garlic powder*
- ☐ *1/4 cup carrot juice*
- ☐ *1/4 cup tomato paste*
- ☐ *1/4 cup water*

- *1/4 teaspoon black pepper, freshly ground*
- *2 cloves garlic, peeled, minced*
- *2 teaspoons Worcestershire sauce*
- *3/4 cup onion, finely diced*
- *13 tablespoons olive oil, divided*

Directions:

1. Preheat 350F.

2. Grease a 12-cup muffin tin with the olive oil, 1 tablespoon each tin.

3. In a medium skillet over medium heat, heat the 1 tablespoon olive oil. Put in the onions, mushrooms, and peppers. Sauté for about 2 minutes. Remove from the heat. Allow to cool.

4. In a small mixing bowl, combine the mustard, tomato paste, Worcestershire sauce, garlic, rosemary, and pepper.

5. In a large mixing bowl, mix the sautéed vegetables, beef, eggs, thyme, and the garlic powder. Stir in 1/2 of the mustard mixture. Combine thoroughly.

6. Spoon the mixture into the greased muffin tin. Bake for about 10 minutes.

7. Meanwhile, combine the remaining 1/2 mustard mixture, carrot juice, and the water in a saucepan. Over medium-high heat, bring to a quick boil, then reduce the heat, simmer covered, until the muffins are taken from the oven.

8. After 10 minutes, remove from the oven. Brush or spoon the sauce over each muffin.

9. Return the muffin in the oven. Bake for about 15 minutes more or until the internal temperature is 160F. Allow the muffins to stand for about 5 minutes before serving.

Cheesy Ham Stromboli

This recipe is great finger food that can also be made ahead of time. Cut the Stromboli into 4 large pieces or into 8 small slices and bake to cheesy and crispy perfection. Serve with roasted broccoli and butter for a delicious breakfast.

Prep Time: 20 minutes; **Cook Time:** 20 minutes

Serving Size: 155 g; **Serves:** 4; **Calories:** 488

Total Fat: 38.6 g **Saturated Fat**: 22.3 g; **Trans Fat:** 0 g

Protein: 26.8 g; **Net Carbs:** 6.2 g

Total Carbs: 11.9 g; **Dietary Fibre:** 5.7 g; **Sugars:** 3.4 g

Cholesterol: 108 mg; **Sodium:** 762 mg; **Potassium:** 366 mg;

Vitamin A: 11%; **Vitamin C:** 6%; **Calcium:** 48%; **Iron:** 37%

Ingredients:

- ☐ *4 ounces ham*
- ☐ *4 tablespoons almond flour*

- ☐ *3 tablespoons coconut flour*
- ☐ *3 1/2 ounces cheddar cheese*
- ☐ *1 1/4 cups mozzarella cheese, shredded*
- ☐ *1 large egg*
- ☐ *1 teaspoon Italian seasoning*
- ☐ *Salt and pepper, to taste*

Directions:

1. Preheat the oven to 400F.

2. In a mixing bowl, combine the coconut flour, the almond flour, and the rest of the seasoning.

3. In a microwave, melt the mozzarella cheese. Heat for about 1 minute, then in 10 seconds interval afterward, stirring occasionally. You can also melt it in a toaster oven for about 10 minutes.

4. When the mozzarella cheese has melted, allow cooling down for a little bit. Add it to the flour mixture. Add in the egg. Combine everything until the mixture becomes a moist dough. Transfer into a flat surface lined with parchment paper.

5. Place the second sheet of parchment paper over the dough. With a rolling pin or your hand, flatten the dough.

6. With a knife or a pizza cutter, cut diagonal lines from the dough edges towards the center, leaving a row of uncut dough, about 4 inches wide.

7. On the uncut surface of the dough, lay the ham and then cheddar. Layer alternately.

8. One section of the cut dough at a time, lay it over the top of the filling, covering it; bake for about 15–20 minutes or until it has turned to a golden brown. Slice and serve.

Prosciutto Frittata Muffins

You won't be able to resist these muffins. This tasty version is wrapped in crispy prosciutto. They are very satisfying and are high in fat, protein, and vitamin A.

Prep Time: 25 minutes; **Cook Time:** 20 minutes

Serving Size: 112 g (1 muffin); **Serves:** 4-6; **Calories:** 147

Total Fat: 11.7 g **Saturated Fat:** 6.2 g; **Trans Fat:** 0 g

Protein: 7.7 g; **Net Carbs:** 2.5 g

Total Carbs: 3.6 g; **Dietary Fibre:** 1.1 g; **Sugars:** 1.4 g

Cholesterol: 132 mg; **Sodium:** 213 mg; **Potassium:** 329 mg;

Vitamin A: 45%; **Vitamin C:** 13%; **Calcium:** 5%; **Iron:** 8%

Ingredients:

- ☐ *8 eggs, large*
- ☐ *5 ounces Prosciutto di Parma*
- ☐ *6 tablespoons ghee or fat of choice, divided, plus more if needed*
- ☐ *3 garlic cloves, minced*
- ☐ *2 tablespoons coconut flour*
- ☐ *1/4 cup coconut milk*
- ☐ *1/2 pound spinach, frozen, thawed, squeezed dry*
- ☐ *1/2 pound cremini mushrooms, thinly sliced*
- ☐ *1/2 medium onion, finely diced*
- ☐ *1 cup cherry tomatoes, halved*
- ☐ *Black pepper, freshly grounded*
- ☐ *Kosher salt*

Directions:

1. Preheat the oven to 375F.

2. In a large cast iron skillet, heat 3 tablespoons of the ghee. Put in the onions. Sauté until translucent and soft.

3. Add in the garlic and the mushrooms. Cook until the moisture of the mushroom have evaporated. Season with salt and pepper. Spoon into a plate. Allow to cool to room temperature.

4. In a large mixing bowl, beat the coconut milk, flour, salt, and pepper until well combined. Add in the cooked mushrooms and the spinach. Stir to combine.

5. Grease a 12-cup muffin tin with the remaining ghee. Line each cup with prosciutto, making sure the bottom and the sides are covered completely.

6. Spoon frittata mixture into each cup. Top each muffin with some cherry tomatoes.

7. Bake for about 20 minutes, rotating the tray 180 degrees halfway through.

8. When baked, allow to cool in the muffin tin for a few minutes, then transfer to wire rack to cool completely.

Chicken, Bacon, and Avocado Cheese Sandwich

This super simple sandwich uses keto cloud bread or Oopsie Rolls. This version of the famous classic BLT is high in fat, more flavorful, and has a delicious texture that you won't forget.

Prep Time: 10 minutes; **Cook Time:** 35 minutes

Serving Size: 360 g; **Serves:** 2; **Calories:** 628

Total Fat: 49.2 g **Saturated Fat:** 24.3 g; **Trans Fat:** 0 g

Protein: 36.1 g; **Net Carbs:** 8.4 g

Total Carbs: 11.6 g; **Dietary Fibre:** 3.2 g; **Sugars:** 4.7 g

Cholesterol: 414 mg; **Sodium:** 942 mg; **Potassium:** 720mg;

Vitamin A: 50%; **Vitamin C:** 32%; **Calcium:** 30%; **Iron:** 16%

Ingredients:

- [ ] *3 ounces cream cheese*
- [ ] *3 large eggs*
- [ ] *1/8 teaspoon cream of tartar*
- [ ] *1/4 teaspoon salt*
- [ ] *1/2 teaspoon garlic powder*

For the filling:

- [ ] *3 ounces chicken*
- [ ] *2 slices pepper jack cheese*
- [ ] *2 slices bacon*
- [ ] *2 grape tomatoes, sliced*

- ☐ *1/4 medium (about 2 ounces) avocado, mashed*
- ☐ *1 teaspoon sriracha*
- ☐ *1 tablespoon mayonnaise*
- ☐ *1 tablespoon ghee*

Directions:

1. Preheat the oven to 300F.

2. Line a baking sheet with parchment paper. Set aside.

3. Separate the egg whites and the egg yolks into 2 dry, clean bowls.

4. Into the bowl of egg bowls, add the cream of tartar and salt. With an electric mixer, whip the egg whites until foamy, soft peaks form.

5. In another mixing bowl, combine the cream cheese and the egg yolk. Beat until the mixture turns pale yellow.

6. Gently fold the egg white mixture into the egg yolk mix, 1/2 at a time.

7. Spoon about 1/4 cup of the mixture. With a spatula, press gently into the mixture, forming squares. Repeat the process with the remaining batter until you make 6 squares. Bake for about 25 minutes.

8. Meanwhile, in a skillet, cook the bacon. When cooked, transfer to a plate.

9. Season the chicken with salt and pepper. In the same skillet, add the ghee. Add the chicken and cook. When cooked, transfer to a plate.

10. Combine the Sriracha and the mayonnaise.

11. When the bread is baked, spread the Sriracha mayo over 1 side of bread. Top with the chicken.

12. Top with a pepper jack slice and then top with a bacon slice. Top with tomato slices. Spread 1/2 of the mashed avocado over. Season according to taste. Top with bread. Repeat the process with the remaining ingredients.

Crunchy Eggplant

Made with gluten-free, low carb ingredients, the crispy eggplant makes for a satisfying ketogenic meal. This recipe is also great as a snack or side dish. Coated with pork rind crumbs, the eggplant is deliciously flavorful with a nice crispy, cheesy texture.

Prep Time: 30 minutes; **Cook Time:** 20-30 minutes

Serving Size: 244 g; **Serves:** 4; **Calories:** 528

Total Fat: 44.9 g **Saturated Fat:** 19.9 g; **Trans Fat:** 0 g

Protein: 22.7 g; **Net Carbs:** 4.2 g

Total Carbs: 10.3 g; **Dietary Fibre:** 6.1 g; **Sugars:** 5.1 g

Cholesterol: 116 mg; **Sodium:** 683 mg; **Potassium:** 381 mg;

Vitamin A: 1%; **Vitamin C:** 6%; **Calcium:** 2%; **Iron:** 14%

Ingredients:

☐ *1 cup pork rind crumbs*

- [ ] *1 large egg*
- [ ] *1 medium-size globe eggplant*
- [ ] *1/2 cup bacon grease, or more as needed*
- [ ] *1/4 cup coconut flour*
- [ ] *2 teaspoons water*
- [ ] *Salt*

Directions:

1. Cut the eggplant into about 1/4-inch slices. Lightly sprinkle both sides of the slices with salt. Allow to sit for about 20-30 minutes.

2. Put the coconut flour on a plate. Beat the eggs and water together. Pour in a concave plate. On another plate, put the pork rind crumbs. Arrange in that order.

3. Heat the bacon grease in a heavy skillet over medium heat.

4. Pat dry the eggplant slices. Dredge an eggplant in the coconut flour, then coat it with the egg wash, and then coat with the pork rind crumbs.

5. Fry the eggplant in hot grease until both sides are crisp and brown. Add more grease as needed. Serve hot topped with fried eggs.

Cream Cheese Oopsie Rolls

These rolls are also known as Keto Cloud Bread and is a low-carb staple. They are versatile, and you can make a large batch and store them in the freezer or the fridge for up to 6 days.. Oopsie rolls are practically flour-less and almost carb-free. You can use them as bread or burger buns. Compared to real bread, Oopsie Rolls are spongier and softer, more like a thick, savory crepe. They taste neutral, so Oopsie Rolls are the perfect bread substitute!

Prep Time: 20 minutes; **Cook Time:** 30 minutes

Serving Size: 39 g (per 1 roll); **Serves:** 3 (2 rolls each); **Calories:** 85

Total Fat: 7.4 g **Saturated Fat:** 3.9 g; **Trans Fat:** 0 g

Protein: 4.2 g; **Net Carbs:** 0.6 g

Total Carbs: 0.6 g; **Dietary Fibre:** 0 g; **Sugars:** 0 g

Cholesterol: 109 mg; **Sodium:** 104 mg; **Potassium:** 60 mg;

Vitamin A: 6%; **Vitamin C:** 0%; **Calcium:** 2%; **Iron:** 4%

Ingredients

- ☐ *3 large eggs*
- ☐ *1 dash of salt*
- ☐ *1 pinches of cream of tartar*
- ☐ *3 ounces of cream cheese*

Directions:

1. Preheat oven to 300 degrees.

2. Separate the eggs, add salt, and cream cheese to the egg yolks. Combine ingredients together.

3. In a separate bowl, whip egg whites and cream of tartar until stiff.

4. Using a spatula, fold the egg yolk mixture into the egg white mixture.

5. Spray a cookie sheet with a non-stick spray and spoon the mixture onto the sheet. Flatten each mound slightly.

6. Bake for 30 minutes.

7. Cool on the baking sheet for a few minutes, then move to a cooling rack and allow Oopsie rolls to totally cool. Store in a bread sack or ziplock bag to keep rolls from drying out.

Sweet Potato, Chicken, Chorizo Sausage Hash

Hash and eggs are meant for each other, especially when the egg is runny, soaking into the hash. The chorizo gives this meal a taste of freshness, with a bit of a kick.

Prep Time: 15 minutes; **Cook Time:** 45 minutes

Serving Size: 226 g; **Serves:** 5; **Calories:** 468

Total Fat: 36.1 g **Saturated Fat**: 11.1 g; **Trans Fat**: 0 g

Protein: 25 g; **Net Carbs:** 8 g

Total Carbs: 9.8 g; **Dietary Fibre:** 1.8 g; **Sugars:** 3.4 g

Cholesterol: 128 mg; **Sodium:** 986 mg; **Potassium:** 654 mg;

Vitamin A: 7%; **Vitamin C**: 32%; **Calcium**: 3%; **Iron**: 18%

Ingredients:

- ☐ *1 egg*
- ☐ *1 large sweet potato; dice*
- ☐ *1 pound chicken sausage*
- ☐ *1 tablespoon (or more as needed) olive oil*
- ☐ *1 zucchini; dice*
- ☐ *1/2 cup (or more as needed) chicken broth*
- ☐ *1/4 teaspoon cayenne pepper*
- ☐ *2 teaspoons garlic powder*
- ☐ *4 ounces chorizo sausage*
- ☐ *To taste: Salt and ground black pepper*

Directions:

1. In a skillet, heat olive oil over medium flame. Put the chorizo sausage and the chicken sausage in the skillet. Cook the sausages for about 10 minutes, stirring until cooked through and brown. Remove excess grease.

2. Into the same skillet where the sausages are cooked, add the diced sweet potato, cayenne pepper, garlic powder, salt, and black pepper. Stir.

3. Pour in the chicken broth. Simmer for 10–15 minutes or until the sweet potato is tender. Add more chicken broth if the mix becomes too dry. Remove excess liquid when the sweet potato is cooked.

4. Pour about 2–3 inches of water into a large saucepan. Bring water to a boil. When boiling, reduce the heat to medium-low. Keep the water gently simmering.

5. Into a small bowl, crack the egg. Hold the bowl just above the surface of the gently simmering water and then gently add the egg. Poach for about 2 1/2 minutes, until the whites are firm, and the yolk is thick but not hard. Using a slotted spoon, remove the poached eggs from the water. Top the poached eggs over the sausage sweet potato mixture.

Butternut Squash Porridge

This is a dairy-free and gluten-free recipe. Butternut squash is pumpkin's cousin. However, it has a higher beta-carotene level. It is also packed with B vitamins and minerals.

Prep Time: 10 minutes; **Cook Time:** 50 minutes

Serving Size: 286 g; **Serves:** 3; **Calories:** 430

Total Fat: 36.2 g **Saturated Fat:** 22.9 g; **Trans Fat**: 0 g

Protein: 3.5 g; **Net Carbs:** 23.5 g

Total Carbs: 29.0 g; **Dietary Fibre:** 5.5 g; **Sugars:** 5.8 g

Cholesterol: 76 mg; **Sodium**: 13 mg; **Potassium**: 891 mg;

Vitamin A: 514%; **Vitamin C**: 83%; **Calcium**: 12%; **Iron**: 12%

Ingredients:

- 1/4 cup (or more to taste) coconut milk
- 1/2 teaspoon ground cinnamon
- 1 tablespoon walnuts, chopped
- 1 butternut squash; cut in half and seed
- Water as needed
- 7 tablespoons ghee

Directions:

1. Preheat oven to 350F (175C).

2. With the cut-side up, place the butternut squash halves into a baking dish.

3. Fill the dish with 1/4 inch water. Place in oven. Bake for about 50–60 minutes, until softened. Cool, the cooked butter squash.

4. Scoop the cooked squash into a bowl. Mash using a potato masher or fork until smooth. Add ghee; stir to combine well.

5. Pour the coconut milk and add the cinnamon into the bowl of mashed squash. Stir. Top with walnuts.

Curried Broccoli Slaw and Pork Frittata

With the curry powder and the pork, this breakfast meal is so flavorful that you won't notice that it doesn't have cheese. Plus, the kids won't notice it contains a lot of veggies. This dish is also wonderful when served with roasted Brussel sprouts.

Prep Time: 15 minutes; **Cook Time:** 45 minutes

Serving Size: 173 g; **Serves:** 6; **Calories:** 345

Total Fat: 27.1 g **Saturated Fat**: 19.9 g; **Trans Fat:** 0 g

Protein: 21.6 g; **Net Carbs:** 4 g

Total Carbs: 5.6 g; **Dietary Fibre:** 1.6 g; **Sugars:** 2.1 g

Cholesterol: 205 mg; **Sodium:** 140 mg; **Potassium:** 468mg;

Vitamin A: 57%; **Vitamin C**: 32%; **Calcium:** 5%; **Iron:** 13%

Ingredients:

- ☐ *6 eggs, large*
- ☐ *3/4 pound pork, ground*
- ☐ *1 cup broccoli slaw, shredded*
- ☐ *4 garlic cloves, minced*
- ☐ *1/4 cup Italian parsley, roughly chopped*
- ☐ *1/4 cup coconut milk*
- ☐ *1/2 onion, thinly sliced*
- ☐ *3/4 cup carrots, shredded*
- ☐ *1 tablespoon curry powder*
- ☐ *6 tablespoons coconut oil*
- ☐ *Black pepper, freshly ground*
- ☐ *Kosher salt*

Directions:

1. Preheat the broiler to 350F.

2. In an 8-inches cast iron skillet, heat the coconut oil. Put the onions and a dash of salt. Sauté until the onions are soft.

3. Add in the pork and the garlic. Stir-fry until the meat is no longer pink. While the pork and the onions are cooking, whisk the eggs, coconut milk, curry powder, salt, pepper, and parsley together.

4. Add in the carrots and the broccoli slaw into the skillet. Season with salt and pepper.

5. Pour the egg mixture into the skillet. Cook for about 5 minutes or until the bottom is set.

6. Transfer the skillet into the broiler. Cook for about 20-30 minutes or until the frittata is puffy, the edges are browned, and a toothpick comes out clean when inserted in the center.

Chapter III

Lettuce Wrapped Egg Salad Sandwich

This high-fat, high protein, the low-carb meal is great to take to work. You can enjoy this as a snack, or you can serve this as a barbecue side dish.

Prep Time: 10 minutes; **Cook Time:** 0 minutes

Serving Size: 99 g; **Serves:** 4; **Calories:** 371

Total Fat: 28.4 g **Saturated Fat:** 9 g; **Trans Fat:** 0 g

Protein: 25.4 g; **Net Carbs:** 2.1 g

Total Carbs: 2.1 g; **Dietary Fibre:** 0 g; **Sugars:** 0.6g

Cholesterol: 186 mg; **Sodium**: 1551 mg; **Potassium**: 373 mg;

Vitamin A: 4%; **Vitamin C**: 1%; **Calcium**: 3%; **Iron**: 8%

Ingredients:

- [ ] *2 lettuce leaves*
- [ ] *3 eggs*
- [ ] *6 cooked bacon*
- [ ] *1 tablespoon mayonnaise*
- [ ] *1 teaspoon Dijon mustard*
- [ ] *1 teaspoon lemon juice*
- [ ] *¼ teaspoon salt*

Directions:

1. Cook the eggs gently in a medium saucepan.

2. Bring to a boil for ten minutes. Remove from heat and cool.

3. Peel the eggs under cold running water.

4. Add the eggs to a food processor and pulse until chopped.

5. Stir in the mayonnaise, mustard, lemon juice, and salt and pepper.

6. Taste and adjust as necessary.

7. Serve with lettuce leaves and bacon for wrapping, if desired.

Chicken Liver and Garlic Pate

This pate recipe is very easy to make. For as little as 5 ingredients and 20 minutes, you can make this low carb dish. This spread is very high in selenium, vitamin A, and B12 and high in iron, pantothenic acid, phosphorus, and riboflavin. This pate is cheap, and there is no strong organ flavor. They can be made ahead for a fast lunch.

Prep Time: 5 minutes; **Cook Time:** 15 minutes	
Serving Size: 297 g; **Serves:** 5; **Calories:** 425	
Total Fat: 33.6 g **Saturated Fat**: 20 g; **Trans Fat**: 0.1 g	
Protein: 23.7 g; **Net Carbs:** 7.4 g	
Total Carbs: 8.7 g; **Dietary Fibre:** 1.3 g; **Sugars:** 3.2 g	
Cholesterol: 421 mg; **Sodium**: 406 mg; **Potassium**: 479 mg;	
Vitamin A: 182%; **Vitamin C**: 37%; **Calcium**: 27%; **Iron**: 45%	

Ingredients:

- ☐ *300 g chicken livers*
- ☐ *3 cucumbers, sliced into rounds, for serving*
- ☐ *2 cloves garlic, crushed*
- ☐ *150 g cheese, cut into 1/4-inch thick pieces, for serving*
- ☐ *120 g butter*
- ☐ *1 tablespoon cracked black peppercorns*
- ☐ *Salt to, taste*

Directions:

1. Wash the chicken livers, pat them dry with kitchen paper. Cut the livers into halves. Trim and remove the sinew or fatty pieces using scissors.

2. In a saucepan, melt the butter over low heat. Add the garlic; gently fry until cooked.

3. Add the livers; cook for about 10 minutes, occasionally stirring.

4. Remove from the heat. Add to the blender; puree using the blade attachment until smooth.

5. Stir in the peppercorns and season with the salt to taste.

6. Pour the liver puree into ramekin dishes and refrigerate until set.

7. Serve with the cucumber rounds and cheese squares, spreading the pate over each piece.

Notes:

These can be kept in the refrigerator for up to 5 days.

Crab Louie

This recipe is also known as Crab Louis or the King of Salads and the original version dates as far as in the early 1900s and is believed to have originated on the West Coast of America. The more crab meat, the better!

Prep Time: 10 minutes; **Cook Time:** 0 minutes

Serving Size: 424 g; **Serves:** 4; **Calories:** 461

Total Fat: 41.2 g **Saturated Fat**: 6.7 g; **Trans Fat**: 0 g

Protein: 22.4 g; **Net Carbs:** 13.7 g

Total Carbs: 18 g; **Dietary Fibre:** 4.3 g; **Sugars:** 6.5 g

Cholesterol: 218 mg; **Sodium:** 918 mg; **Potassium:** 562 mg;

Vitamin A: 42%; **Vitamin C**: 32%; **Calcium:** 36%; **Iron:** 40%

Ingredients:

- ☐ *6 cups lettuce leaves or salad greens*
- ☐ *4 eggs, hard-boiled, sliced into halves*

- 1/4 cup minced chives
- 1/2 cup of your favorite Louisiana Rémoulade Dressing
- 3/4 pound lump crab meat, cooked
- 1 pound asparagus, trimmed
- 1 cup cherry tomatoes
- 6 tablespoons vegetable oil

Directions:

1. In a pot of boiling salted water, blanch the asparagus for about 1 minute. Immediately transfer blanched asparagus into a bowl of cold water. When the asparagus is cool, drain the water and toss with the vegetable oil.

2. Divide the lettuce into 4 plates. Arrange the crabmeat, the asparagus, tomatoes, and hard-boiled eggs into the 4 plates. Garnish with chives. Serve with the rémoulade on the side.

Bacon Bleu Zoodle Salad

What can be a better combo than bacon and blue cheese? This low-carb, high-fat salad is very easy to make and is packed with protein, vitamins, and minerals. This delicious summer salad can be served with your favorite low-carb barbecue.

Prep Time: 15 minutes; **Cook Time:** 0 minutes

Serving Size: 282 g; **Serves:** 2; **Calories:** 246

Total Fat: 21.8 g **Saturated Fat:** 4.1 g; **Trans Fat:** 0.6 g

Protein: 5.1 g; **Net Carbs:** 8.4 g

Total Carbs: 11.2 g; **Dietary Fibre:** 2.8 g; **Sugars:** 5.1g

Cholesterol: 7 mg; **Sodium**: 481 mg; **Potassium**: 692 mg;

Vitamin A: 32%; **Vitamin C**: 72%; **Calcium**: 8%; **Iron**: 7%

Ingredients

- ☐ *4 cups of zucchini noodles*
- ☐ *1 cup of fresh spinach*
- ☐ *1/3 cup of chunky blue cheese dressing (the fatter, the better!)*
- ☐ *½ cup crumbled bacon*
- ☐ *Cracked pepper to taste*

Directions

1. Just toss everything together and eat! Yum!

Lettuce Wrapped Tuna-Avocado

Simple yet flavorful tuna and avocado salad is a healthy, light lunch recipe that can also be enjoyed as an appetizer or snack. Here's a fun fact: not only are lettuce leaves a healthier option than bread, these leaves keep teeth white, and the iron in lettuce helps form an acid-resistant barrier in your mouth, which protects your enamel from damage!

Prep Time: 15 minutes; **Cook Time:** 0 minutes

Serving Size: 153 g (per wrap); **Serves:** 1; **Calories:** 285

Total Fat: 23.4 g **Saturated Fat:** 10.4 g; **Trans Fat:** 0 g

Protein: 14.4 g; **Net Carbs:** 8.4 g

Total Carbs: 7.8 g; **Dietary Fibre:** 4.2 g; **Sugars:** 0.9 g

Cholesterol: 52 mg; **Sodium:** 136 mg; **Potassium:** 489 mg;

Vitamin A: 12%; **Vitamin C:** 22%; **Calcium:** 2%; **Iron:** 4%

Ingredients:

- [ ] *2 butter lettuce leaves*
- [ ] *1/2 medium avocado*
- [ ] *1/2 lime*
- [ ] *1/2 jalapeño, diced small*
- [ ] *1 scallion, thinly sliced*
- [ ] *4 ounces wild albacore tuna, canned in water, drained*
- [ ] *2 tablespoons ghee*
- [ ] *Black pepper, freshly ground*
- [ ] *Kosher salt*

Directions:

2. Put the tuna in a medium sized bowl. With a fork, gently break the fish into pieces.

3. Add the scallions and the jalapeño. Toss well.

4. Add in the ghee, salt, and pepper. Squeeze a spritz of lime. Mix.

5. In a separate bowl, mash half an avocado with salt, pepper, and the rest of the lime juice. Add into the tuna mixture. Stir to combine. Divide the tuna salad mixture into 2 portions. Place into the lettuce leaves. Wrap and eat up.

Avocado Tuna Melt Bites

These high-fat, high protein, low carb bites have a creamy, soft filling on the inside and a crispy texture on the outside. Enjoy these with your favorite low carb salad for a perfect low carb lunch.

Prep Time: 15 minutes; **Cook Time:** 5 minutes

Serving Size: 172 g; **Serves:** 4; **Calories:** 574

Total Fat: 51.7 g **Saturated Fat:** 27.8 g; **Trans Fat:** 0 g

Protein: 21.6 g; **Net Carbs:** 3.6 g

Total Carbs: 7.8 g; **Dietary Fibre:** 4.2 g; **Sugars:** 0.9 g

Cholesterol: 26 mg; **Sodium:** 143 mg; **Potassium:** 545 mg;

Vitamin A: 3%; **Vitamin C:** 9%; **Calcium:** 3%; **Iron:** 6%

Ingredients:

- ☐ 10 ounce. canned tuna drained
- ☐ 1/4 cup mayonnaise
- ☐ 1 medium avocado, cubed
- ☐ 1/4 cup Parmesan cheese
- ☐ 1/3 cup almond flour
- ☐ 1/2 tsp. garlic powder
- ☐ 1/4 tsp. onion powder
- ☐ Salt and pepper to taste
- ☐ 1/2 cup coconut oil

Directions:

1. Drain tuna and add it to a large mixing bowl.

2. Add mayonnaise, Parmesan cheese, and spices to the tuna and mix.

3. Slice the avocado in half, remove the pit and cube the insides.

4. Add avocado into the tuna mixture and fold together. Try not to mash the avocado! Form the tuna mixture into balls.

5. Roll in almond flour, covering completely.

6. Heat coconut oil in a pan over medium heat.

7. Add tuna balls and fry until crisp on all sides.

8. Remove from the pan and serve.

Keto Taco Salad

This easy version of the Mexican taco is a salad that may become your favorite go-to recipe. With sour cream and salsa on the side, you can pack the taco mixture easily and take it with you for lunch.

Prep Time: 10 minutes; **Cook Time:** 10 minutes	
Serving Size: 202 g; **Serves:** 6; **Calories:** 511	
Total Fat: 40.5 g **Saturated Fat:** 16.9 g; **Trans Fat:** 0 g	
Protein: 32.2 g; **Net Carbs:** 3.9 g	
Total Carbs: 4.5 g; **Dietary Fibre:** 0.6 g; **Sugars:** 1.3 g	
Cholesterol: 112 mg; **Sodium:** 534 mg; **Potassium:** 510 mg;	
Vitamin A: 14%; **Vitamin C:** 2%; **Calcium:** 35%; **Iron:** 9%	

Ingredients:

- [ ] *16 ounce. ground pork*
- [ ] *9 ounce. cheddar cheese, shredded*

- *6 tsp McCormick taco seasoning*
- *8 tablespoon vegetable oil*
- *12 tablespoon sour cream*
- *12 tablespoon salsa*
- *6 romaine leaves*
- *Cayenne pepper to taste*

Directions:

1. Brown the pork in a skillet with the oil.

2. Once the meat is browned, add taco seasoning and any additional spices.

3. Cook until the taco seasoning is incorporated.

4. Let cool, and then distribute into 6 containers.

5. Add cheese to each container.

6. Add sour cream and salsa to a prep bowl and plastic wrap it.

7. Add Romaine lettuce to the container.

Dill and Garlic Cauliflower Steaks

These vegetable steaks are seared in the pan and then roasted until are tender. Flavored with dill and garlic, they are a great light main dish or a hearty side dish.

Prep Time: 5 minutes; **Cook Time:** 20 minutes	
Serving Size: 135 g; **Serves:** 4-6; **Calories:** 130	
Total Fat: 11.4 g **Saturated Fat:** 1.7 g; **Trans Fat:** 0 g	
Protein: 2.6 g; **Net Carbs:** 3.9 g	
Total Carbs: 7.2 g; **Dietary Fibre:** 3 g; **Sugars:** 2.9 g	
Cholesterol: 0 mg; **Sodium:** 68 mg; **Potassium:** 383 mg;	
Vitamin A: 1%; **Vitamin C:** 95%; **Calcium:** 4%; **Iron:** 5%	

Ingredients:

- ☐ *1 medium head cauliflower, stems and leaves removed*
- ☐ *1 tablespoon fresh dill, chopped (or more, if you like)*
- ☐ *3 garlic cloves, minced*
- ☐ *4 tablespoon olive oil, divided*
- ☐ *Juice of 1/2 lemon (about 2 tablespoons)*
- ☐ *Salt and pepper, to taste*

Directions:

1. Preheat the oven to 400F.

2. With the stem side down, place the cauliflower on a

cutting board. Slice the cauliflower into 4-6 pieces 1-inch thick steaks. Start by cutting the head into halves. Cut each half into 2-3 steaks, making 4-6 steaks in the process. If you get any random florets, save them and cook along with the steaks.

3. In a large-sized skillet, heat 2 tablespoons of olive over medium-high heat. Arrange the cauliflower slices in the skillet; cook for about 2 minutes per side until dark spots begin to appear.

4. Transfer the cauliflower slices into a baking sheet. In a small-sized bowl, stir the remaining 2 tablespoons olive oil, lemon juice, garlic, and dill. Brush the mixture or spoon them over the cauliflower steaks; sprinkle with the salt and pepper to taste.

5. Roast the cauliflower for about 15 minutes or until just tender. Serve.

Keto Pizza

This cauliflower-powered pizza is grain-free and gluten-free. This low-carb recipe folds up just like the traditional version, and you can pick each slice by your hand. Feel free to add more high-fat, low-carb toppings.

Prep Time: 15 minutes; **Cook Time:** 10 minutes	
Serving Size: 187 g; **Serves:** 4; **Calories:** 217	
Total Fat: 30.1 g **Saturated Fat:** 7.6 g; **Trans Fat:** 0 g	
Protein: 10.7 g; **Net Carbs:** 12.4 g	
Total Carbs: 18 g; **Dietary Fibre:** 5.6 g; **Sugars:** 9.2 g	
Cholesterol: 53 mg; **Sodium:** 444 mg; **Potassium:** 676 mg;	
Vitamin A: 12%; **Vitamin C**: 115%; **Calcium**: 20%; **Iron**: 9%	

Ingredients for the base:

- ☐ *1 cauliflower*
- ☐ *1 1/4 grated mozzarella*
- ☐ *32 g grated Parmesan*
- ☐ *1 egg*
- ☐ *1 tsp minced garlic*
- ☐ *1 tsp oregano*

For the pizza sauce:

- ☐ *250 g Italian pasta sauce*
- ☐ *1 teaspoon chili infused tomato puree*
- ☐ *1 teaspoon oregano*
- ☐ *1 teaspoon minced garlic*

- [ ] *A few fresh basil leaves*
- [ ] *7 tablespoons vegetable oil*

For the topping:

- [ ] *1 small ball of fresh mozzarella*
- [ ] *Handful of grated mozzarella*
- [ ] *Toppings can be whatever else you fancy! I went for sliced tomatoes, mushrooms, and sliced black olives*

Directions:

1. Grate your cauliflower until it resembles fine grains of rice. When done, put the 'rice' in the microwave for 4 minutes. Strain to get rid of any moisture.

2. Put your cheeses, egg and seasoning in a large mixing bowl. Mix, the cauliflower to the cheese and egg, creating your keto pizza dough.

3. Use a pizza pan to form the base.

4. Cook in a 350-degree oven for about 10 minutes.

5. Mix the sauce ingredients, spread over the baked cauliflower crust.

6. Add your toppings in whichever way you like. Place in oven for five more minutes.

7. Invite your friends and family over!

Paleo Mayonnaise

This version of mayo can be made without a blender. Plus, if you use the same amount of bacon fat in place of the avocado oil, you'll have an even fatter version with that salty, smoky, bacon taste. You can call it baconnaise. Compared to store-bought mayo, homemade mayo is fluffier, lighter, more alive, and richer.

Prep Time: 5 minutes; **Cook Time:** 20 minutes

Serving Size: 15 g; **Makes:** 3/4 cup (9 tablespoons); **Calories:** 87

Total Fat: 9 g **Saturated Fat:** 1.5 g; **Trans Fat:** 0 g

Protein: 1.2 g; **Net Carbs:** 0.7 g

Total Carbs: 1.7 g; **Dietary Fibre:** 1 g; **Sugars:** 0.5 g

Cholesterol: 23 mg; **Sodium:** 69 mg; **Potassium:** 45 mg;

Vitamin A: 1%; **Vitamin C:** 1%; **Calcium:** 1%; **Iron:** 3%

Ingredients:

- ☐ *1 large egg yolk*
- ☐ *1 1/2 teaspoons fresh lemon juice*
- ☐ *1 teaspoon distilled white vinegar*
- ☐ *1/4 teaspoon Dijon-style mustard*
- ☐ *1/4 teaspoon kosher salt*
- ☐ *3/4 cup macadamia nut or avocado oil*

Directions:

1. In a medium bowl, whisk the yolk, mustard, salt, vinegar, and lemon juice for about 30 seconds or until the egg yolk thickens, and the color of the mix

brightens.

2. In a slow, steady stream, pour about 1/3 of the oil into the bowl, vigorously mixing the mix for about 1 minute.

3. After the oil is well combined, add another 1/3 of the oil while whisking.

4. Then add the remaining oil, whisking until you have a thick mayonnaise.

5. Enjoy with your favorite paleo sandwiches.

Cheesy Bacon Wrapped Hot Dogs

Here is another very simple yet super delicious low carb lunch that you can eat for dinner, too! These dogs are very rich, savory, and fatty.

Serves: 8

Prep. Time: 10 minutes

Cook Time: 20 minutes

Prep Time: 10 minutes; **Cook Time:** 20 minutes
Serving Size: 105 g; **Makes:** 8; **Calories:** 379
Total Fat: 30.5 g **Saturated Fat:** 16.1 g; **Trans Fat:** 0 g
Protein: 23.1 g; **Net Carbs:** 1.9 g
Total Carbs: 1.9 g; **Dietary Fibre:** 0 g; **Sugars:** 0.7 g
Cholesterol: 91 mg; **Sodium:** 912 mg; **Potassium:** 205 mg;
Vitamin A: 12%; **Vitamin C:** 2%; **Calcium:** 41%; **Iron:** 2%

Ingredients:

- ☐ *8 sausage links*
- ☐ *8 strips bacon*
- ☐ *16 slices pepper jack cheese*
- ☐ *Black pepper*
- ☐ *Garlic powder*
- ☐ *Onion powder*
- ☐ *Paprika*

Directions:

1. Cook sausage links on a grill until they're just almost done.

2. Let them cool.

3. Cut a slit in the middle of the sausage links.

4. Place 2 slices of cheese into the middle of each dog.

5. Wrap each dog tightly in bacon. Secure with wet toothpicks to make sure the bacon doesn't shrivel and open up the dog.

6. Sprinkle with your spices and grill on your BBQ grill until the bacon is crispy (about 15–20 minutes). Flip halfway through.

7. Place on plate with low-carb sides and eat away!

Monte Cristo Sandwich

The traditional version of this sandwich is made with 2 slices of French toast, turkey, ham, and Swiss cheese. Sometimes, it is fried and served with maple syrup for dipping. Not what we have here but delicious none the less! This recipe is low-carb, high–fat, high protein, and packed with calcium.

Prep Time: 15 minutes; **Cook Time:** 15 minutes

Serving Size: 200 g; **Makes:** 4; **Calories:** 632

Total Fat: 49.7 g **Saturated Fat:** 16.5 g; **Trans Fat:** 0 g

Protein: 37.5 g; **Net Carbs:** 7.1 g

Total Carbs: 10.4 g; **Dietary Fibre:** 3.3 g; **Sugars:** 2.1 g

Cholesterol: 273 mg; **Sodium:** 718 mg; **Potassium:** 531 mg;

Vitamin A: 14%; **Vitamin C:** 2%; **Calcium:** 51%; **Iron:** 27%

Ingredients:

- ☐ *4 large eggs*
- ☐ *¾ cup almond flour*
- ☐ *¼ cup coconut oil or ghee*
- ☐ *2 teaspoons vanilla extract*
- ☐ *2 tablespoons Erythritol*
- ☐ *½ teaspoon baking soda*
- ☐ *1 teaspoon cream of tartar*
- ☐ *4 slices of turkey (maple cured is great)*

For the filling:

- ☐ *4 slices ham (rosemary or smoked ham is awesome)*

- [ ] *2 cups shredded Swiss cheese*
- [ ] *Low-carb / sugar-free syrup*

Directions:

1. Crack eggs into a bowl and beat until totally mixed.

2. Add dry ingredients, continue mixing, and add a splash of water if the mixture is too thick.

3. Grease a pan with coconut oil. Using a ladle, make four pancakes.

4. Cook on low heat for five minutes or until the top of the pancakes start to firm up. Flip to the other side and cook for another minute or two.

5. Once the pancakes are ready, separate the turkey and ham into four piles with two slices each.

6. Two piles of turkey with two slices, and two piles of ham with two slices.

7. Add 1/2 cup of Swiss cheese to each pile.

8. Cook on medium-low in the same pan that you cooked the pancakes, add a little more coconut oil, and cover with a lid until the cheese is melted.

9. Serve with sugar-free or low-carb syrup.

Tuna Burgers

These patties make for easy and quick weekday lunch meals. Adding olive oil to the mixture makes sure that they do not get dry. Tuna contains omega 3 fatty acids and is a good way to get a dose of heart-healthy oil.

Serves: 4

Prep Time: 20 minutes; **Cook Time:** 10 minutes	
Serving Size: 203 g; **Makes:** 4; **Calories:** 544	
Total Fat: 37.4 g **Saturated Fat:** 6.9 g; **Trans Fat:** 0 g	
Protein: 37.4 g; **Net Carbs:** 7.1 g	
Total Carbs: 3.8 g; **Dietary Fibre:** 1.6 g; **Sugars:** 1.1 g	
Cholesterol: 158 mg; **Sodium:** 556 mg; **Potassium:** 545 mg;	
Vitamin A: 6%; **Vitamin C:** 6%; **Calcium:** 6%; **Iron:** 11%	

Ingredients:

- ☐ *1 tablespoon ginger root, grated*
- ☐ *1/2 cup almond meal*
- ☐ *1/4 cup cilantro, chopped*
- ☐ *2 cans (8-ounce) tuna; drain*
- ☐ *2 tablespoons lemon juice*
- ☐ *4 tablespoons olive oil*
- ☐ *2 tablespoons soy sauce*
- ☐ *3 eggs*
- ☐ *kosher salt and ground black pepper to taste*
- ☐ *For frying: 3 tablespoons olive oil*

Directions:

1. Except for the olive oil for frying, mix all the ingredients by hand or using a food processor until the ingredients are well incorporated, and the mix becomes firm in consistency.

2. Divide the mix into four equal portions and form into patties.

3. In a skillet or grill pan, heat the 1 tablespoon of olive oil over medium heat.

4. Cook the tuna burgers for about five minutes each side or until the patties and set and the sides are browned.

5. Enjoy with your favorite paleo-friendly burger bun with avocado, lettuce, and tomato.

Nutty Vegetable Patties

These delicious low carb, vegetable burgers are addictive. The seeds give the patties fantastic texture and crunch with a nutty taste. They are gluten-free with only veggies as ingredients. Enjoy them between your favorite low carb burger bun with avocado, lettuce, and tomato.

Prep Time: 15 minutes; **Cook Time:** 15 minutes

Serving Size: 76 g; **Makes:** 4; **Calories:** 196

Total Fat: 17.2 g **Saturated Fat:** 1.6 g; **Trans Fat:** 0 g

Protein: 6.5 g; **Net Carbs:** 7.1 g

Total Carbs: 7.7 g; **Dietary Fibre:** 3.2 g; **Sugars:** 1.5 g

Cholesterol: 0 mg; **Sodium:** 300 mg; **Potassium:** 303 mg;

Vitamin A: 51%; **Vitamin C:** 35%; **Calcium:** 5%; **Iron:** 7%

Ingredients:

- [ ] 2/3 cup mashed butternut squash, cut into 1/2-inch cubes for steaming
- [ ] 1/2 cup cauliflower, chopped
- [ ] 1/2 cup broccoli, chopped
- [ ] 1/8 teaspoon ground black pepper
- [ ] 1/4 teaspoon ground cumin
- [ ] 1/4 cup sunflower seed kernels, raw
- [ ] 1/4 cup almonds, raw
- [ ] 1/2 teaspoon salt
- [ ] 1/2 cup walnuts, raw
- [ ] 1 tablespoon vegetable oil

Directions:

1. Into a saucepan, place a steamer insert. Fill the saucepan with water just below the bottom of the steamer. Bring the water to a boil. Add the butternut squash cubes. Steam for about 7–10 minutes or until tender. Transfer the cooked squash into a bowl and then mash. Measure 1/2 cup of mashed butternut squash, reserve.

2. Return the steamer insert into the saucepan. Refill with water just below the bottom of the steamer. Bring water to boil. Add in the broccoli and the cauliflower. Cover and steam for about 2-6 minutes until tender. When cooked, transfer the cauliflower to a bowl. Set aside.

3. Blend the almonds, walnuts, and sunflower seeds

together in a food processor or a blender until it resembles coarse breadcrumbs. Add in the cooked broccoli and cauliflower. Blend until all the ingredients are finely chopped and well mixed. Add in the 1/2 cup mashed squash, cumin, salt, and pepper. Blend until well incorporated. If the mix is too thick to mix, transfer the ingredients into a bowl and mix hand.

4. Divide the mix into four equal portions and form into patties. In a large skillet, heat oil over medium-high heat.

5. Cook the patties about 2 minutes each side, until heated through and browned. Enjoy with your favorite Paleo-friendly burger bun with avocado, lettuce, and tomato.

Stir-Fried Kale with Bacon

This yummy one-pan recipe is fast and super easy to make. The bacon and vinegar perfectly balance the taste of the wilted bitter kale. You will love this delicious shortcut to enjoying your greens.

Prep Time: 10 minutes; **Cook Time:** 20 minutes

Serving Size: 170 g; **Makes:** 2; **Calories:** 472

Total Fat: 37.4 g **Saturated Fat**: 10.6 g; **Trans Fat**: 0 g

Protein: 23.7 g; **Net Carbs:** 8.7 g

Total Carbs: 10 g; **Dietary Fibre:** 1.3 g; **Sugars:** 0 g

Cholesterol: 62 mg; **Sodium:** 1427 mg; **Potassium:** 756 mg;

Vitamin A: 26%; **Vitamin C:** 181%; **Calcium:** 12%; **Iron:** 12%

Ingredients:

☐ *4 ounces (about 1/2 cup) bacon, cut into 1/4-inch strips*

- ☐ 1 bunch (about 6 ounces) kale, leaves removed, thinly chopped
- ☐ 2 tablespoons vegetable oil
- ☐ A squeeze of lemon
- ☐ Black pepper, freshly ground
- ☐ Kosher salt

Directions:

1. In a large cast iron skillet, sauté the bacon bits with the oil over medium heat until they are crisp.

2. Add in the kale. Season with a dash of salt and pepper.

3. Stir the bacon and the kale for a few minutes. Add a splash of vinegar. Serve with a squeeze of lemon.

Salade Lyonnaise

This version of the classic French bistro salad is a delicious low carb recipe. The bitter greens tossed with warm vinaigrette and topped cooked bacon, and poached eggs will tickle your taste buds.

Prep Time: 10 minutes; **Cook Time:** 20 minutes

Serving Size: 118 g; **Makes:** 2; **Calories:** 201

Total Fat: 16.3 g **Saturated Fat:** 7.1 g; **Trans Fat:** 0 g

Protein: 11.3 g; **Net Carbs:** 1.4 g

Total Carbs: 2.1 g; **Dietary Fibre:** 0.7 g; **Sugars:** 1.2 g

Cholesterol: 194 mg; **Sodium:** 444 mg; **Potassium:** 290 mg;

Vitamin A: 27%; **Vitamin C:** 10%; **Calcium:** 9%; **Iron:** 9%

Ingredients:

- ☐ *2 eggs, poached*
- ☐ *2 tablespoons balsamic vinegar*
- ☐ *4 cups baby arugula*
- ☐ *4 slices bacon, cross-cut into 1/4-inch pieces*
- ☐ *1 tablespoon ghee*
- ☐ *Black pepper, freshly ground*
- ☐ *Kosher salt*

Directions:

1. In a single layer, arrange the bacon slices in a large cast-iron skillet. Over medium heat, cook for about 15-20 minutes or until crunchy.

2. Meanwhile, if you don't have poached eggs, make them.

3. When the bacon is cooked, transfer to a paper towel-lined plate.

4. When the bacon fat has slightly cooled, carefully pour into a heat resistant measuring cup or bowl. Add the ghee and the balsamic vinegar into the bacon fat. Briskly stir to mix. This will be the bacon dressing.

5. Put the arugula into a salad bowl. Pour in as much bacon dressing as you desire. Toss to evenly distribute the dressing. Season with the salt and the pepper to taste.

6. Divide the salad into large bowls or plates. Top each serve with a poached egg and crispy bacon. Serve immediately.

Chicken Salad Basilica

This recipe is another great way to enjoy your cauliflower rice. Who said you couldn't enjoy cauliflower for more than rice substitute? This new low carb meal is versatile, and you can find more to incorporate cauliflower rice in your keto life.

Prep Time: 10 minutes; **Cook Time:** 20 minutes

Serving Size: 180 g; **Makes:** 2; **Calories:** 414

Total Fat: 37.1 g **Saturated Fat:** 6.6 g; **Trans Fat:** 0 g

Protein: 17.1 g; **Net Carbs**: 1.4 g

Total Carbs: 7 g; **Dietary Fibre**: 2.2 g; **Sugars**: 2.1 g

Cholesterol: 37 mg; **Sodium**: 390 mg; **Potassium**: 293 mg;

Vitamin A: 9%; **Vitamin C**: 32%; **Calcium**: 17%; **Iron**: 10%

Ingredients:

- ☐ *1/2 cup chicken, cooked, diced*
- ☐ *2 tablespoons sun-dried tomatoes, packed in olive oil, chopped*
- ☐ *2 tablespoons red wine vinegar*
- ☐ *2 tablespoons pine nuts*
- ☐ *2 tablespoons Parmesan cheese, shredded*
- ☐ *1/4 head cauliflower, the bottom stems trimmed, cut into chunks*
- ☐ *1/4 cup red onion, diced*
- ☐ *1/4 cup olives, chopped (half green and half black)*
- ☐ *1/4 cup olive oil, extra-virgin*
- ☐ *1/4 cup fresh basil, minced*
- ☐ *1 garlic clove, crushed*
- ☐ *Black pepper, ground*
- ☐ *Salt*
- ☐ *Water*

Directions:

1. Put the garlic into a small bowl. Pour in the olive oil. Allow to sit while you assemble the salad

2. Put the cauliflower into the food processor and shred until rice grain size. Transfer into a microwavable

bowl with a cover. Add a couple of teaspoons of water. Cover the bowl; microwave for 4–5 minutes on high. When the microwave beeps, immediately remove the cover to stop further cooking. Drain the excess water and transfer into a large mixing bowl. Allow to cool for a couple of minutes.

3. In a small skillet over low heat, stir in the pine nuts until they are lightly golden. Add the basil, onion, olives, tomatoes, chicken, and pine nuts into the cauliflower bowl. Pour the garlic-infused olive oil over. Stir everything to mix.

4. Add in the vinegar. Stir everything again; season with salt and pepper to taste.

5. Divide the salad between 2 plates. Top each serve with the Parmesan cheese.

Stir Fried Napa Cabbage with Mushrooms and Bacon

This tasty dish is very easy to make. This lovely lunch is so flavorful you might want to add this to your family cookbook!

Prep Time: 10 minutes; **Cook Time:** 30 minutes

Serving Size: 370 g; **Makes:** 4; **Calories:** 479

Total Fat: 37.9 g **Saturated Fat:** 10.5 g; **Trans Fat:** 0 g

Protein: 26.1 g; **Net Carbs:** 6.6 g

Total Carbs: 9.4 g; **Dietary Fibre:** 2.8 g; **Sugars:** 4.2 g

Cholesterol: 62 mg; **Sodium:** 1537mg; **Potassium:** 1142 mg;

Vitamin A: 188%; **Vitamin C:** 160%; **Calcium:** 24%; **Iron:** 16%

Ingredients:

- ☐ *8 ounces cremini mushrooms, thinly sliced*
- ☐ *8 ounces (about 1 cup) bacon, diced*
- ☐ *1 small head (about 840 g) Napa cabbage, sliced crosswise into 1/2-inch pieces*
- ☐ *1/4 cup chicken broth*
- ☐ *1 small onion, thinly sliced*
- ☐ *4 tablespoons vegetable oil*
- ☐ *Salt*
- ☐ *Pepper*

Directions:

1. Heat a large cast iron skillet over medium heat. Put in

the bacon. Sauté until cooked and crispy. Transfer to a plate and crumble. Set aside.

2. In the same skillet, add in the onions. Season with salt and pepper. Cook until translucent and soft.

3. Add the mushrooms. Season with salt and pepper. Sauté until the moisture has evaporated.

4. Add in the Napa cabbage. Pour the chicken broth. Cover with the skillet lid. Reduce the heat to medium-low. Simmer for about 5–10 minutes or until the cabbage is tender according to preference. Adjust the seasoning. Sprinkle the seasoned bacon.

Spinach with Bacon, Mushrooms, and Shallots

Well, you have probably noticed by now how we love to add bacon to our greens. And you probably also discovered that everything is better with bacon. It certainly packs a flavorful punch to sautéed spinach.

Prep Time: 10 minutes; **Cook Time:** 30 minutes	
Serving Size: 450 g; **Makes:** 2; **Calories:** 415	
Total Fat: 33.4 g **Saturated Fat**: 12.6 g; **Trans Fat:** 0 g	
Protein: 14.5 g; **Net Carbs:** 6.6 g	
Total Carbs: 17.1 g; **Dietary Fibre:** 6 g; **Sugars:** 3.9 g	
Cholesterol: 38 mg; **Sodium**: 454 mg; **Potassium**: 2119 mg;	
Vitamin A: 428%; **Vitamin C**: 108%; **Calcium**: 26%; **Iron**: 40%	

Ingredients:

☐   *12 ounces cremini mushrooms, sliced*

- ☐ *1 pound baby spinach, organic*
- ☐ *3 slices uncured bacon, baked and crumbled*
- ☐ *2 teaspoons vinegar*
- ☐ *2 large shallots, thinly sliced*
- ☐ *4 tablespoons bacon grease, reserved from cooked bacon*
- ☐ *Black pepper, freshly ground*
- ☐ *Kosher salt*

Directions:

1. In a cast iron, over medium heat, heat the bacon grease. When hot, sauté the shallots with a dash of salt and pepper until they are soft and translucent.

2. Add in the mushrooms. Cook until they are browned and the mushroom liquid is evaporated.

3. In batches, toss in the spinach, adding more as they wilt; season with vinegar, salt, and pepper.

4. Plate the dish. Sprinkle with the bacon bits.

Grilled Herbed Portobello

Marinated with herbs, these grilled mushrooms are a tasty meaty dish. The mushrooms absorb all the delicious flavors of the oregano, thyme, garlic, and balsamic vinegar. Serve as a main course, sliced over a salad, or as a side dish.

Prep Time: 20 minutes; **Cook Time:** 10 minutes

Serving Size: 109 g; **Makes:** 4; **Calories:** 118

Total Fat: 10.7 g **Saturated Fat:** 1.5 g; **Trans Fat:** 0 g

Protein: 2.2 g; **Net Carbs:** 6.6 g

Total Carbs: 5.1 g; **Dietary Fibre:** 1.5 g; **Sugars:** 1.6 g

Cholesterol: 0 mg; **Sodium:** 297 mg; **Potassium:** 426 mg;

Vitamin A: 0%; **Vitamin C:** 1%; **Calcium:** 2%; **Iron:** 5%

Ingredients:

- ☐ *4 pieces fresh Portobello mushroom caps*
- ☐ *3 tablespoons olive oil*
- ☐ *3 tablespoons balsamic vinegar*
- ☐ *2 cloves garlic, minced*
- ☐ *1/2 teaspoon salt*
- ☐ *1/2 teaspoon dried thyme*
- ☐ *1/2 teaspoon dried oregano*
- ☐ *1/4 teaspoon dried rosemary*
- ☐ *Fresh black pepper*

Directions:

1. Scrape out the gills from under the mushrooms caps using a spoon. Trim the stem.

2. Except for the mushrooms, add all the ingredients in a resealable bag; seal and shake to mix well.

3. Add the mushrooms in the bag; seal and shake, making sure to coat all the sides of the caps. Marinate for 1 hour in the refrigerator. The mushrooms will absorb the marinade.

4. Heat the grill to medium-high.

5. Remove the mushrooms from the marinade; grill for about 10 to 15 minutes, turning once, until done.

Big-O Burger

Warning: This burger is dangerously delicious. Your family and friends will be coming over to your house all the time for them. The bacon and the added mushrooms give the patties a powerful blast of flavors. Eat them wrapped in lettuce, or if you have time, roasted Portobello mushroom caps.

Prep Time: 30 minutes; **Cook Time:** 10 minutes

Serving Size: 221 g; **Makes:** 4; **Calories:** 470

Total Fat: 35.9 g **Saturated Fat:** 9.2 g; **Trans Fat:** 0 g

Protein: 30.5 g; **Net Carbs:** 6.6 g

Total Carbs: 5.1 g; **Dietary Fibre:** 0.7 g; **Sugars:** 1.9 g

Cholesterol: 82 mg; **Sodium:** 1571 mg; **Potassium:** 897 mg;

Vitamin A: 0%; **Vitamin C:** 0%; **Calcium:** 2%; **Iron:** 64%

Ingredients:

- ☐ *4 ounces bacon, frozen, cross-cut into small pieces*
- ☐ *1 pound ground beef*
- ☐ *6 tablespoons vegetable oil, divided*
- ☐ *1/2 pound cremini mushrooms, minced*
- ☐ *1 1/2 teaspoons kosher salt*
- ☐ *Black pepper, freshly ground*

Directions:

1. In a cast-iron skillet over medium heat, heat 1 tablespoon of the ghee. Put the mushrooms. Sauté until the liquid has evaporated. Set aside and allow to cool to room temperature.

2. Put the bacon in the food processor, pulse until ground meat in texture.

3. In a large mixing bowl, combine the mushrooms, bacon, and ground beef. Season with the salt and pepper.

4. With your hands, gently combine the ingredients, making sure not to overwork the meat.

5. Divide the mixture into 4 portions. Form each portion into balls and flatten into 3/4 –inch patties.

6. In a cast iron skillet over medium heat, heat the remaining 1 tablespoon oil. Cook the patties for about 3 minutes each side, turning once.

7. When cooked, transfer to a wire rack to cool. Serve with your choice burger toppings, Portobello mushroom buns, or wrap them in lettuce leaves.

Avocado Fries

This is a new and exciting way to enjoy heart-healthy avocadoes. These are very high in fat.

Prep Time: 20 minutes; **Cook Time:** 20 minutes

Serving Size: 165 g; **Makes:** 4; **Calories:** 518

Total Fat: 50.3 g **Saturated Fat:** 10.7 g; **Trans Fat:** 0 g

Protein: 10.4 g; **Net Carbs:** 3.5 g

Total Carbs: 11.7 g; **Dietary Fibre:** 8.2 g; **Sugars:** 1.2 g

Cholesterol: 89 mg; **Sodium:** 169 mg; **Potassium:** 604 mg;

Vitamin A: 7%; **Vitamin C:** 17%; **Calcium:** 14%; **Iron:** 8%

Ingredients:

- ☐ *2 ripe but firm avocados*

- ☐ *2 eggs*

- ☐ *1/2 cup almond flour, more as needed*

- ☐ *1/2 cup parmesan cheese, grated, more as needed*

- ☐ *6 tablespoons vegetable oil, or preferred frying oil, more if necessary*

- ☐ *Salt, to taste*

Directions:

1. Cut the avocados into halves. Remove the seeds. With a spoon, remove the avocado meat from the leathery skin, making sure to keep the meat intact.

2. With the flat side down, place the avocado halves on a cutting board. Cut the halves lengthwise into 3/4-inch thick slices.

3. Beat the eggs in the bowl until the mixture is uniform.

4. Place the almond flour in a deep plate.

5. Place the parmesan cheese in another plate.

6. Coat the avocado slices with the flour, dip in the egg batter, then coat with the cheese. The best way to do this is to coat all the slices in the flour first, then dip them all in the egg batter, and finally coating them all in cheese, making sure the batter is coated with the cheese.

7. Heat the oil in the frying pan. When the oil is hot, add the avocadoes; fry until both sides are brown, flipping if necessary using tongs. When both sides are browned, set on a paper towel-lined plate. This will keep them from being soggy and absorb excess oil.

8. Alternatively, place them on a well-greased cookie sheet; bake in preheated oven at 400-425F for about 15 to 20 minutes or until browned and crispy.

9. These are best served hot.

Notes:

Make sure you use firm ripe avocadoes to make them easier to handle.

Cauliflower Fried Rice

Cauliflower Rice is a game changer. Gone are the days when you have to count calories every time you eat a dish with rice. This keto version is a no-guilt Shortcut to Ketosis. This lunch is all vegetables, but you won't know the difference since it tastes like Chinese fried rice. Plus, if you have kids, they won't know they are eating cauliflower.

Prep Time: 15 minutes; **Cook Time:** 30 minutes

Serving Size: 176 g; **Makes:** 4; **Calories:** 217

Total Fat: 17.5 g **Saturated Fat:** 9.4 g; **Trans Fat:** 0 g

Protein: 8.7 g; **Net Carbs:** 3.5 g

Total Carbs: 8.5 g; **Dietary Fibre:** 2.9 g; **Sugars:** 3.4 g

Cholesterol: 131 mg; **Sodium:** 711 mg; **Potassium:** 449 mg;

Vitamin A: 15%; **Vitamin C:** 58%; **Calcium:** 5%; **Iron:** 13%

Ingredients:

- ☐ 4 ounces mushrooms, sliced
- ☐ 3 slices bacon, uncured, cut into small dice
- ☐ 2 tablespoons cilantro leaves, chopped
- ☐ 2 tablespoons basil, chopped
- ☐ 2 scallions, thinly sliced
- ☐ 2 large eggs
- ☐ 1-inch knob ginger grated
- ☐ 1-2 tablespoons coconut amino
- ☐ 1 tablespoon mint, chopped
- ☐ 1 small onion, minced
- ☐ 1 small head cauliflower, separated into florets
- ☐ 4 tablespoons ghee
- ☐ Black pepper, freshly ground
- ☐ Kosher salt

Optional:

- ☐ Splash of fish sauce
- ☐ Splash of coconut vinegar

Directions:

1. Put the cauliflower in a food processor. Process until the size of rice.

2. In a large cast iron skillet, cook the bacon over medium heat until crispy. When cooked, transfer to a plate, leaving the grease in the skillet.

3. While the bacon is cooking, whisk the eggs in a small mixing bowl with some salt and pepper to taste. Pour

into the skillet and cook until well done. When cooked, transfer to a plate and slice thinly. Set aside.

4. Increase the heat to medium-high. Put in the onion. Season with a dash of salt and pepper. Cook until soft.

5. Add in the mushrooms. Sprinkle with a dash of salt and pepper. Stir-fry until browned.

6. Add in the ginger. Cook stirring for about 30 seconds.

7. Add in the cauliflower. Season with a dash of salt and pepper.

8. Put the lid of the skillet. Lower the heat to low. Cook for about 5 minutes or until the cauliflower is tender but not mushy. Remove from the heat.

9. Add in the coconut amino, herbs, and the eggs. If desired, add a splash of coconut vinegar and fish sauce.

10. Add the bacon in. Toss everything together.

Salmon, Spinach, and Feta Burger

These patties are a healthy alternative to the traditional burger. They are made from simple ingredients, and they come out moist. Be sure not to process your fish and spinach too much. You want them chunky for the patties. Serve with your low carb buns or muffin with a spread of avocado sauce.

Prep Time: 10 minutes; **Cook Time:** 6 minutes	
Serving Size: 135 g; **Makes:** 4 (1-2 per serve); **Calories:** 255	
Total Fat: 20.2 g **Saturated Fat:** 9.1 g; **Trans Fat:** 0 g	
Protein: 16.9 g; **Net Carbs:** 3.5 g	
Total Carbs: 2.8 g; **Dietary Fibre:** 1.4 g; **Sugars:** 0.7 g	
Cholesterol: 67 mg; **Sodium:** 150 mg; **Potassium:** 452 mg;	
Vitamin A: 26%; **Vitamin C:** 13%; **Calcium:** 9%; **Iron:** 5%	

Ingredients:

- ☐ *1 pound salmon*
- ☐ *2 ounces spinach (roughly chopped if large leaf, fine as if baby)*
- ☐ *2 ounces feta, crumbled*
- ☐ *1 1/2 tablespoons lemon juice*
- ☐ *4 tablespoons ghee*
- ☐ *Pepper, to taste*

For the sauce:

- ☐ *1/2 avocado*
- ☐ *4 tablespoons sour cream*
- ☐ *4 teaspoons lemon juice*
- ☐ *1 medium garlic clove, crushed or minced*

For serving:

- ☐ *Buns or muffins (about 3-6 depending on the number of servings)*

Directions:

1. Remove the skins from the salmon. Inspect the meat and make sure there are no bones, cut into 2-inch cubes.

2. Put the salmon cubes in a food processor. Add the spinach; process the salmon and the spinach are broken and combined, but the mixture is not mushy. Transfer to a bowl.

3. Add the feta, ghee, lemon juice, and generous grinding of pepper. Mix until everything is well combine, making sure the cheese is spread through the mix. Divide the mixture into 6 portions; form into burgers. The patties will be soft. If you have time, lay them on a tray and chill in the freezer to set them before cooking.

4. Fry of the grill with as little oil for about 3 minutes per side of until cooked through and gently browned.

5. While cooking, prepare the sauce. Mash the avocado. Add the rest of the ingredients of the sauce and mix to

combine.

6. Toast the low carb muffins or buns. Spread a thin layer of avocado cream and top with the burger.

Tasty Tomato Soup

You'll dive in head first to taste this creamy soup. It's so delicious you won't believe it's easy to make and low carb. The tomatoes and the aroma of the fresh basil come together beautifully fresh and vibrant. The tomatoes pack this soup with lycopene, which helps rid of free radicals that damage the cells of our body.

Prep Time: 15 minutes; **Cook Time:** 40 minutes	
Serving Size: 519 g; **Makes:** 4; **Calories:** 319	
Total Fat: 25.5 g **Saturated Fat**: 7.5 g; **Trans Fat:** 0 g	
Protein: 7 g; **Net Carbs:** 13.6 g	
Total Carbs: 18.4 g; **Dietary Fibre:** 4.8 g; **Sugars:** 10.6 g	
Cholesterol: 0 mg; **Sodium:** 613 mg; **Potassium:** 940 mg;	
Vitamin A: 143%; **Vitamin C**: 63%; **Calcium**: 9%; **Iron**: 9%	

Ingredients:

- ☐ *5 large tomatoes; chop roughly*
- ☐ *3 garlic cloves; minced*
- ☐ *3 cups vegetable or chicken broth*
- ☐ *6 tablespoon vegetable oil*
- ☐ *2 carrots; chop roughly*
- ☐ *1 tablespoon tomato paste*
- ☐ *1 large white onion; chop roughly*
- ☐ *¼ cup fresh basil, chopped*
- ☐ *¼ cup coconut milk*

To taste:

- ☐ *Sea salt*
- ☐ *Freshly ground black pepper*

Directions:

1. In a large saucepan, heat cooking oil over medium heat.

2. Add the onion in and the carrot. Cook for about 10 minutes or until soft.

3. Add in the garlic. Cook for about 1-2 minutes more.

4. Add in the tomatoes, the tomato paste, the basil, and the chicken broth. Season with salt and pepper. Stir to combine ingredients.

5. Bring to boil. Adjust heat to low, simmer uncovered for about 30 minutes.

6. Pour in the coconut milk. Blend the soup directly in the pan using an immersion blender or blend using a food processor until smooth.

Tuna-Topped Gazpacho

This healthy dish that is quick to prepare and with minimum clean-up afterward is perfect for a weekday lunch. For added flavor, season with freshly chopped parsley or basil.

Prep Time: 10 minutes; **Cook Time:** 2 hours

Serving Size: 434 g; **Serves:** 2; **Calories:** 1070

Total Fat: 108.1 g **Saturated Fat:** 15.9 g; **Trans Fat:** 0 g

Protein: 7 g; **Net Carbs:** 13.6 g

Total Carbs: 18.4 g; **Dietary Fibre:** 4.8 g; **Sugars:** 10.6 g

Cholesterol: 26 mg; **Sodium:** 193 mg; **Potassium:** 764 mg;

Vitamin A: 42%; **Vitamin C:** 100%; **Calcium:** 4%; **Iron:** 7%

Ingredients:

- ☐ *1 can (6 ounces or more to taste) tuna; drain and flake*
- ☐ *1 cup olive oil*
- ☐ *1 teaspoon (or more to taste) hot sauce (I use Frank's Red Hot)*
- ☐ *1/2 cucumber; chop roughly*
- ☐ *1/2 green bell pepper*
- ☐ *2 cloves garlic (or more to taste); peel*
- ☐ *2 sweet (or more to taste) tomatoes; cut into halves*
- ☐ *To taste: 1 pinch salt and ground black pepper*

Optional:

- ☐ *Fresh chopped parsley or basil*

☐ *1 tablespoon water as needed*

Directions:

1. In a high-powered blender, combine the cucumber, tomatoes, and garlic. Blend for about 10–30 seconds or until smooth.

2. Add the hot sauce, olive oil, salt and pepper. Blend for about 5–15 seconds or until smooth.

3. If the mixture is too thick, add about 1 tablespoon water at a time and blend until smooth.

4. Add the bell pepper. Blend for about 1–2 seconds until the bell pepper is finely chopped but not liquefied.

5. Chill the gazpacho for at least two hours before serving. Top with tuna and freshly chopped parsley or basil. You can make ahead of time for a quick lunch.

Asparagus Cream Soup

This easy, silky smooth soup is a fresh dish. You can serve it hot or cold with toasted low carb bread with poached egg.

Prep Time: 15 minutes; **Cook Time:** 30 minutes	

Prep Time: 15 minutes; **Cook Time:** 30 minutes

Serving Size: 409 g; **Serves:** 6; **Calories:** 190

Total Fat: 16 g **Saturated Fat:** 9.9 g; **Trans Fat:** 0 g

Protein: 4.5 g; **Net Carbs:** 5.6 g

Total Carbs: 9.7 g; **Dietary Fibre:** 4.1 g; **Sugars:** 4.5 g

Cholesterol: 42 mg; **Sodium:** 614 mg; **Potassium:** 380 mg;

Vitamin A: 35%; **Vitamin C:** 24%; **Calcium:** 8%; **Iron:** 25%

Ingredients:

- ☐ *1 cup water*
- ☐ *1 large yellow onion, chopped (1 1/2 to 2 cups chopped)*
- ☐ *1 tablespoon dry vermouth*
- ☐ *1/4 cup heavy cream*
- ☐ *2 pounds asparagus, trimmed of woody stem bottoms*
- ☐ *2 tablespoons chopped fresh parsley*
- ☐ *4 cups chicken stock*
- ☐ *7 tablespoons unsalted butter*
- ☐ *A squeeze of fresh lemon juice*
- ☐ *Leaves of 2 sprigs of fresh thyme*

☐ *Salt and pepper*

Directions:

1. About 1 1/2 inches from the top of the asparagus, cut the tip of the spears. Cut them lengthwise into halves if they are thick; reserve for garnish. Cut the remaining asparagus stalks into 1/4-inch rounds.

2. Over medium-high, melt the butter in a 4 or 5-quart pot. Add the onions; cook for about 5 minutes or until translucent.

3. Add the chopped asparagus stalks, season with salt and pepper to taste, and cook for 5 minutes more.

4. Add the water, broth, and the thyme. Increase the heat to a boil. When boiling, reduce the heat to a simmer; cover and continue cooking for about 10 to 15 minutes or until the asparagus is tender. At the end of cooking, stir in the parsley.

5. While the soup is cooking, blanch the tips in a small pot of salted water (1 1/2 teaspoons per quart of water) for about 2 to 4 minutes or until the tips are just tender. Drain and rinse under running cool water to stop cooking; set aside.

6. With an immersion blender, blend the soup until the mixture is smooth. Alternatively, you can blend the soup in small batches, about 1/3 of the blender content at a time.

7. Pour the pureed soup through a sieve, pressing if needed.

8. Stir in the cream, the vermouth, and the lemon juice; season with salt and pepper to taste. Divide into

serving bowls and garnish with the asparagus tips.

Chapter IV

Dinner Recipes

Broccoli and Beef

This classic Chinese dish is easy and quick to make. This homemade version is even better than the restaurant version.

Prep Time: 15 minutes; **Cook Time:** 15 minutes

Serving Size: 183 g; **Serves:** 6; **Calories:** 301

Total Fat: 23.6 g **Saturated Fat:** 4.7g; **Trans Fat:** 0 g

Protein: 13.8 g; **Net Carbs:** 5.6 g

Total Carbs: 8.9 g; **Dietary Fibre:** 2.3 g; **Sugars:** 1.4 g

Cholesterol: 21 mg; **Sodium:** 719 mg; **Potassium:** 395 mg;

Vitamin A: 9%; **Vitamin C:** 103%; **Calcium:** 7%; **Iron:** 11%

Ingredients:

- ☐ *1/2 pound flank steak, cut into 1/4-inch-thick pieces*
- ☐ *1 tablespoon soy sauce*
- ☐ *1 tablespoon rice wine vinegar*
- ☐ *4 1/2 cups (about 1 medium head broccoli) broccoli florets, chopped*
- ☐ *8 tablespoons peanut oil*
- ☐ *2 cloves garlic, peeled and minced*

- ☐ *Optional garnishes: and*
- ☐ *Sesame seeds toasted*
- ☐ *Green onions, thinly sliced*

For the sauce:

- ☐ *1 tablespoon cornstarch*
- ☐ *1 tablespoon rice wine vinegar*
- ☐ *1 teaspoon sesame oil*
- ☐ *1/4 teaspoon black pepper, freshly ground*
- ☐ *1/4 teaspoon ground ginger*
- ☐ *3 tablespoons oyster sauce*
- ☐ *3 tablespoons soy sauce*
- ☐ *3/4 cup water*
- ☐ *Optional: 1 to 3 teaspoons sriracha, to taste*

Directions:

1. Put the steak in a large-sized bowl. Add the rice wine vinegar and soy sauce; stir to combine. Marinate for at least 10 minutes or up to 1 hour.

2. Meanwhile, fill a large pot halfway full of water; bring to a boil. Stir in the broccoli florets; cook for about 30 to 45 minutes. Drain and set aside.

3. Prepare the sauce. Whisk all of the ingredients together until well combined.

4. Add the peanut oil in a large-sized sauté pan or a wok;

heat over medium-high heat. Add the marinated steaks and garlic; sauté for about 5 to 6 minutes, occasionally stirring, until cooked through.

5. Add the broccoli and the sauce; toss to combine and cook for 1 to 2 minutes more or until the sauce is thick and simmers.

6. Remove from the heat; serve immediately. If desired, garnish.

Steak with Mushroom Port Sauce

What this go- to meal is easy to make and delicious. Just grab some piece of beef, cook it in a skillet, make the sauce in the same skillet, and you have a fancy dinner in almost no time at all. You also get to have fun flambéing the mushrooms.

Prep Time: 10 minutes; **Cook Time:** 5-15 minutes	

Prep Time: 10 minutes; **Cook Time:** 5-15 minutes
Serving Size: 688 g; **Serves:** 2; **Calories:** 1129
Total Fat: 39.3 g **Saturated Fat**: 18 g; **Trans Fat**: 0 g
Protein: 4.5 g; **Net Carbs:** 5.6 g
Total Carbs: 7 g; **Dietary Fibre:** 1.4 g; **Sugars:** 2.9 g
Cholesterol: 462 mg; **Sodium**: 267 mg; **Potassium:** 2045 mg;
Vitamin A: 12%; **Vitamin C**: 7%; **Calcium**: 4%; **Iron**: 107%

Ingredients:

☐   *2 lb rib-eye steak*

- 10 ounce. mushrooms
- 1 tablespoon of grass-fed butter
- Salt and pepper to taste
- 4 ounce. port wine
- 2 ounce. heavy cream

Directions:

1. Preheat oven to 450F.

2. Salt and pepper both sides of the steaks.

3. Use a cast iron skillet and place on stove on high.

4. Melt butter in skillet.

5. Cook steak for 2 minutes per side, and then move to the oven.

6. Cook steak in the oven until internal temperature reaches the desired level of doneness (135 for medium rare).

7. When steaks are done, set aside and cover with tin foil.

8. Next, add some port wine to the pan and scrape off the burnt bits off the bottom.

9. Add mushrooms and cream to the skillet, then use a match to light wine on fire (optional).

10. This will thicken the sauce, then pour over the steak and enjoy.

Pistachio-Crusted Salmon

Did you know that you can prepare a seriously sophisticated dinner within 20 minutes with just 6 ingredients? This recipe doesn't need fancy techniques or fussy ingredients to make it a crowd-pleasing meal.

Prep Time: 5minutes; **Cook Time:** 15 minutes

Serving Size: 329 g; **Serves:** 2; **Calories:** 714

Total Fat: 56.9 g **Saturated Fat:** 9.5 g; **Trans Fat:** 0 g

Protein: 49.2 g; **Net Carbs**: 13.6 g

Total Carbs: 7 g; **Dietary Fibre**: 3.2 g; **Sugars**: 1.5 g

Cholesterol: 100 mg; **Sodium**: 791 mg; **Potassium**: 1108 mg;

Vitamin A: 6%; **Vitamin C**: 3%; **Calcium**: 13%; **Iron**: 16%

Ingredients:

- ☐ *1-pound wild king salmon fillet, skin on, pin bones removed*
- ☐ *2 tablespoon scallions or chives, chopped*
- ☐ *1/2 cup pistachios, shelled, salted, dry roasted, crushed*
- ☐ *6 tablespoons Dijon mustard*
- ☐ *5 tablespoons vegetable oil*
- ☐ *Black pepper, freshly ground*
- ☐ *Kosher salt*

Directions:

1. Preheat the 400F.

2. Line a baking tray with parchment paper.

3. With a paper towel, pat the fish dry. Divide the fillet into 2 uniform pieces. Season the skin with salt and pepper. With the skin-side down, lay it down on the prepared baking tray.

4. In a small mixing bowl, combine the mustard, vegetable oil, and the chives. Spread 1/2 of the mixture evenly on each piece of fish.

5. Sprinkle the crushed nuts on top of the mustard, patting them down gently and making sure they stick.

6. Place the tray in the oven. Bake for about 10-15 minutes or until the salmon is cooked through to your desired doneness.

7. Remove the salmon from the oven. Allow to rest for a couple of minutes.

8. Meanwhile, reheat some leftover vegetables and dice some cherry tomatoes.

Fried Mackerel with Mushroom Sauce

Fresh mackerel is always a winner. The combination of pan-fried mackerel and the mushroom makes a delicious, healthy dinner.

Prep Time: 10 minutes; **Cook Time:** 20 minutes	
Serving Size: 462 g; **Serves:** 4; **Calories:** 904	
Total Fat: 69.5 g **Saturated Fat**: 14.9 g; **Trans Fat**: 0 g	
Protein: 57.9 g; **Net Carbs:** 13.6 g	
Total Carbs: 11.3 g; **Dietary Fibre:** 3.2 g; **Sugars:** 5.7 g	
Cholesterol: 170 mg; **Sodium**: 237 mg; **Potassium**: 1402 mg;	
Vitamin A: 22%; **Vitamin C**: 30%; **Calcium**: 7%; **Iron**: 32%	

Ingredients:

- ☐ *8 ounces (or 240 g) button mushrooms, sliced*
- ☐ *2 tablespoons white wine vinegar*
- ☐ *2 tablespoons almond flour*
- ☐ *2 pounds (or 960 g) mackerel fillets*
- ☐ *2 onions, peeled, finely chopped*
- ☐ *12 ounces (or 360 g) tomatoes, cut into 1/2-inch slices*
- ☐ *1 garlic clove, peeled, crushed*
- ☐ *8 tablespoons vegetable oil*
- ☐ *Salt and freshly ground black pepper*

Directions:

158

1. In a large deep skillet, heat the olive oil. Dip the mackerel in the almond flour. Add the coated fish in the pan and fry each side for 5 minutes. Transfer the fried mackerel into serving the dish and set aside.

2. In the same skillet, add the onion, garlic, and mushrooms; cook for about 10 to 12 minutes, gently stirring, and season with salt and pepper to taste.

3. Stir in vinegar; boil the mixture until it evaporates. Add the tomato; cook for 2 minutes.

4. Spoon the mushroom mixture over the mackerel fillets.

Zoodles with Lamb Meatballs

Zucchini noodles or zoodles are what's in right now. You'll be surprised at how they make an excellent substitute for regular noodles. Use the julienne blade o fa trusty mandoline or a spiralizer. Top your zoodle with this scrumptious meatball recipe and enjoy a high taste, low-carb dinner.

Prep Time: 10 minutes; **Cook Time:** 20 minutes

Serving Size: 306 g; **Serves:** 4; **Calories:** 676

Total Fat: 52.8 g **Saturated Fat:** 12 g; **Trans Fat:** 0 g

Protein: 35 g; **Net Carbs:** 12.2 g

Total Carbs: 15.4 g; **Dietary Fibre:** 3.2 g; **Sugars:** 8.6 g

Cholesterol: 156 mg; **Sodium:** 444 mg; **Potassium:** 833 mg;

Vitamin A: 14%; **Vitamin C:** 20%; **Calcium:** 6%; **Iron:** 23%

Ingredients:

- ☐ *1/2 lb. (1 ounce.) zoodles (zucchini noodles)*
- ☐ *12 ounce. Pasta sauce*
- ☐ *1 lb. Ground lamb*
- ☐ *2 shallots*
- ☐ *1 egg yolk*
- ☐ *1 teaspoon cinnamon*
- ☐ *1 teaspoon cumin*
- ☐ *12 tablespoons vegetable oil*
- ☐ *Cayenne pepper to taste*
- ☐ *Salt and pepper to taste*
- ☐ *Red pepper flakes to taste*

Directions:

1. Preheat oven to 450 degrees.

2. Using a mandolin at the julienne setting, slice the zucchini. You only want the outer parts.

3. Mix the rest of the ingredients together except for the pasta sauce and the olive oil and form 16 meatballs.

4. Cook the meatballs for 12 minutes in the oven.

5. Stir the pasta sauce and oil together. Add the pasta sauce and zoodles into a saucepan and cook for an additional 3–4 minutes.

Basil Chicken with Vegetables

This dinner dish is very high in vitamin C, high in vitamin A, low in sugar, and low in sodium. If you don't want carrots in your meal, add another pepper, thinly sliced, instead of the sliced carrots.

Prep Time: 20 minutes; **Cook Time:** 30 minutes	
Serving Size: 246 g; **Serves:** 4; **Calories:** 471	
Total Fat: 38 g **Saturated Fat:** 7.9 g; **Trans Fat:** 0 g	
Protein: 28.6 g; **Net Carbs:** 4 g	
Total Carbs: 5.8 g; **Dietary Fibre:** 1.8 g; **Sugars:** 3.1 g	
Cholesterol: 71 mg; **Sodium:** 124 mg; **Potassium:** 235 mg;	
Vitamin A: 92%; **Vitamin C:** 98%; **Calcium:** 8%; **Iron:** 7%	

Ingredients:

- ☐ 4 pieces (about 1 pound total) chicken breast halves, skinless, boneless, cut into 1-inch strips

- ☐ 1 large bell pepper, thinly sliced

- ☐ 1 small zucchini, sliced

- ☐ 1/2 cup fresh basil, shredded, tightly packed

- ☐ 1/2 teaspoon freshly ground black pepper

- ☐ 1/4 cup (1 ounce) Parmesan cheese, grated fresh

- ☐ 2/3 cup carrot, thinly sliced

- ☐ 4 tablespoons olive oil, divided

- ☐ 4 tablespoons vegetable oil, divided

Directions:

1. Preheat the oven to 375F.

2. Tear off 4 pieces 12-inch long heavy-duty aluminum foil. Fold the foil pieces into the half, the shiny sides together. Place them on a baking sheet, open them up with the shiny side up, coat each with 1 tablespoon vegetable oil.

3. Divide the chicken into 4 portions, on 1/2 of each foil square near the crease. Divide the vegetables into 4 portions, spoon them over the chicken, sprinkle with the basil, and season with pepper. Drizzle 1 tablespoon of olive oil over each packet. Fold the foil over the chicken and the vegetables, bringing the edge together. Fold the edges of the foil to seal them securely. Pleat and crimp the edges to make the packets airtight; bake for about 30 minutes.

4. Remove the chicken from the packets, transferring them into individual serving plates. Alternatively, you can transfer the packets on individual serving plates. Cut open the top of each packet and fold the aluminum foil back.

Sprinkle each serving with 1 tablespoon of cheese

Turkey Curry in a Hurry

This quick to make dinner meal is a great use for any leftover turkey. This recipe transforms boring leftover meat into an exciting spicy dinner served over cauliflower rice or shirataki noodles.

Prep Time: 10 minutes; **Cook Time:** 20 minutes

Serving Size: 222 g; **Serves:** 6; **Calories:** 476

Total Fat: 37.6 g **Saturated Fat:** 19.5 g; **Trans Fat:** 0 g

Protein: 29.9 g; **Net Carbs:** 4.3 g

Total Carbs: 6.5 g; **Dietary Fibre:** 2.2 g; **Sugars:** 2.9 g

Cholesterol: 71 mg; **Sodium:** 201 mg; **Potassium:** 535 mg;

Ingredients:

- ☐ *4 cups turkey, cooked, diced*
- ☐ *3/4 cup chicken broth, or turkey broth if you have it*
- ☐ *7 tablespoons vegetable oil (or coconut oil)*
- ☐ *2 teaspoons garam masala*
- ☐ *2 garlic cloves, crushed*
- ☐ *1/2 medium onion, chopped*
- ☐ *1 teaspoon ground turmeric*
- ☐ *1 teaspoon ground cinnamon*
- ☐ *1 teaspoon cayenne pepper*
- ☐ *1 tablespoon fresh ginger, grated*
- ☐ *1 3/4 cups (about 410 ml) coconut milk*
- ☐ *Salt*

Directions:

1. In a big, heavy skillet over medium-low heat, add the oil. Add the garam masala, turmeric, and cinnamon. Stir for 1 minute or so.

2. Add in the onions. Sauté until translucent.

3. Add the coconut milk, the chicken broth, ginger, garlic, and cayenne. Stir until the sauce becomes creamy.

4. Stir in the turkey. Adjust the burner to low. Simmer for about 15 minutes.

5. Season with salt to taste. Serve over cauliflower rice or

shirataki noodles.

Salmon with Mango-Avocado Salsa

If you love tropical fruits, you'll crave this recipe! The mango-avocado salsa topped with pan-seared salmon gives this dish a refreshing tangy taste.

Prep Time: 20 minutes; **Cook Time:** 10 minutes	
Serving Size: 250 g; **Serves:** 5; **Calories:** 487	
Total Fat: 38.9 g **Saturated Fat**: 8.4 g; **Trans Fat**: 0 g	
Protein: 27.3 g; **Net Carbs:** 8 g	
Total Carbs: 11 g; **Dietary Fibre:** 3 g; **Sugars:** 6.8 g	
Cholesterol: 73 mg; **Sodium**: 95 mg; **Potassium**: 757 mg;	
Vitamin A: 14%; **Vitamin C**: 28%; **Calcium**: 6%; **Iron**: 6%	

Ingredients:

- ☐ *1 1/2 pounds fresh wild king salmon filet*
- ☐ *2 tablespoons ghee*

- ☐ *Kosher salt*
- ☐ *Black pepper, freshly ground*

For the salsa:

- ☐ *7 tablespoons olive oil, extra virgin*
- ☐ *2 cups (about 2 mangos) ripe mango, diced*
- ☐ *1/4 teaspoon red pepper flakes*
- ☐ *1/4 cup fresh cilantro, minced*
- ☐ *1/2 cup red onion, finely diced*
- ☐ *1 cup (1 medium avocado) Hass avocado, diced*
- ☐ *1 lime, juiced*
- ☐ *Black pepper, freshly ground*

Directions:

For the salmon:

1. Cut the salmon into 5 serving pieces. Pat the fish with a paper towel until very dry. Season all the sides with salt and pepper.

2. In a cast iron skillet over medium-high heat, heat the ghee until simmering.

3. With the skin side down, put in the salmon fillets. Turn down the heat to medium-low. Gently press each fillet down with a flexible spatula to prevent them from curling up and the skin to crisp evenly. Cook for about 6 minutes or until the skin easily comes off the surface of the skillet or the meat thermometer is between 120F–130F. Quickly sear the meat sides for about 30 seconds each. Place on the plate with the

crispy skin on top. Top each serve with salsa.

For the salsa:

1. Put the diced mango in a bowl.

2. Add in the rest of the ingredients. Stir to combine.

3. Adjust the seasoning according to taste; top over the salmon fillets.

Herbed Baked Salmon

This very simple dish is quite an enjoyable dinner. The herbs make this dish burst with buttery flavor. And the vegetables make it a nutritious high-fat, low-carb meal.

Prep Time: 20 minutes; **Cook Time:** 20 minutes	
Serving Size: 171 g; **Serves:** 8; **Calories:** 392	
Total Fat: 32.7 g **Saturated Fat:** 10.3 g; **Trans Fat:** 0 g	
Protein: 24.3 g; **Net Carbs:** 2 g	
Total Carbs: 2 g; **Dietary Fibre:** 0 g; **Sugars:** 0.6 g	
Cholesterol: 80 mg; **Sodium:** 1139 mg; **Potassium:** 516 mg;	
Vitamin A: 14%; **Vitamin C:** 28%; **Calcium:** 6%; **Iron:** 6%	

Ingredients:

- ☐ *2 pounds salmon fillets*
- ☐ *4 ounces sesame oil*
- ☐ *1/2 cup tamari soy sauce*
- ☐ *1 teaspoon minced garlic*
- ☐ *1/2 teaspoon ground ginger*
- ☐ *1/2 teaspoon basil*
- ☐ *1 teaspoon oregano leaves*
- ☐ *1/4 teaspoon thyme*
- ☐ *1/2 teaspoon rosemary*
- ☐ *1/4 teaspoon tarragon*
- ☐ *4 ounces butter*
- ☐ *1/2 cup chopped fresh mushrooms*
- ☐ *1/2 cup chopped green onions*

Directions:

1. Stir together the tamari sauce, sesame oil, and spices. Put the salmon in a plastic bag and pour in the sauce mixture.

2. Refrigerate the salmon, skin side up, in the marinade for 1–4 hours.

3. Preheat oven to 350 degrees F. Line a large baking pan with foil.

4. Pour out the fillets and marinade into the pan. The fish should be in a single layer.

5. Bake fillets for 10–15 minutes.

6. While the salmon is baking, get the vegetables ready.

7. Melt the butter. Add the vegetables to it, and mix to coat vegetables.

8. Remove the salmon from the oven, and pour the butter mixture over the salmon fillets, making sure each fillet is covered.

9. Bake at 350 degrees F for about 10 minutes more. Serve immediately.

Cauliflower Cheeseburger BBQ Bacon Waffles

This recipe is another dish that shows the versatility of cauliflower. Rice, pizza crust, and now we have waffles! You will appreciate this savory recipe. The waffle becomes crispy and complements the salty and sweet taste of the bacon-beef mixture. The cheese on top completes this dinner meal perfectly.

Prep Time: 10 minutes; **Cook Time:** 30 minutes

Serving Size: 266 g; **Serves:** 2; **Calories:** 749

Total Fat: 58.8 g **Saturated Fat:** 21.1 g; **Trans Fat:** 0 g

Protein: 49.2 g; **Net Carbs:** 2 g

Total Carbs: 7.6 g; **Dietary Fibre:** 2.8 g; **Sugars:** 2.5 g

Cholesterol: 310 mg; **Sodium:** 877 mg; **Potassium:** 655 mg;

Vitamin A: 17%; **Vitamin C:** 39%; **Calcium:** 57%; **Iron:** 71%

Ingredients:

For the waffles:

- ☐ *1 cup (about 125g) cauliflower, crumbled*
- ☐ *1 1/2 ounces cheddar cheese*
- ☐ *3 tablespoons Parmesan cheese*
- ☐ *4 tablespoons almond flour*
- ☐ *2 large eggs*
- ☐ *1/4 teaspoon onion powder*
- ☐ *1/4 teaspoon garlic powder*
- ☐ *3 tablespoons vegetable oil*
- ☐ *Salt and pepper, to taste*

For the topping:

- ☐ *4 ounces (70/30) ground beef*
- ☐ *1 1/2 ounces cheddar cheese*
- ☐ *4 slices bacon, chopped*
- ☐ *4 tablespoons BBQ sauce, sugar-free*
- ☐ *Salt and pepper to taste*

Directions:

1. Put the cauliflower into a large mixing bowl. Add in the rest of the waffle ingredients. Mix and set aside.

2. Cut the bacon into thin slices. Cook over medium-high heat until partially done. Add in the beef. Cook the bacon and beef are crispy. Add the excess grease of the cooked bacon and beef into the waffle mixture.

3. Immersion blends the waffle mixture until the texture is a thick paste.

4. Pour half of the waffle iron mixture into the waffle iron. Cook, until there is little or no steam coming out from the waffle iron or the cauliflower waffle, is crisp. Cook the remaining waffle.

5. While the cauliflower waffles are cooking, add the BBQ sauce into the bacon-beef mixture in the pan.

6. For each cauliflower waffle, put in 1/2 of the BBQ bacon-beef mixture and 1/2 of the cheddar cheese.

7. Broil for about 1–2 minutes or until the cheese has melted nicely. Serve immediately. Sprinkle with green onion.

Shrimp-Stuffed Mushrooms

Whenever I serve this dish, there are never any leftovers. They are incredibly delicious bites. The seafood stuffing takes the meaty, rich flavor and texture of the mushrooms to another level of deliciousness!

Prep Time: 20 minutes; **Cook Time:** 20 minutes

Serving Size: 356 g; **Serves:** 3 (8 pieces each); **Calories:** 493

Total Fat: 39 g **Saturated Fat:** 11.6g; **Trans Fat:** 0 g

Protein: 24.8 g; **Net Carbs:** 9.7 g

Total Carbs: 11.4 g; **Dietary Fibre:** 1.7 g; **Sugars:** 4.2 g

Cholesterol: 186 mg; **Sodium:** 502 mg; **Potassium:** 1209 mg;

Vitamin A: 14%; **Vitamin C:** 5%; **Calcium:** 12%; **Iron:** 8%

Ingredients:

- ☐ *8 ounces shrimp, frozen or fresh, thawed if frozen*
- ☐ *24 ounces (about 24 pieces medium-sized) cremini*

174

mushrooms

- [ ] *2 bacon slices (about 1/3 cup), diced*
- [ ] *2 tablespoons ghee*
- [ ] *1/4 cup scallions (about 2 scallions), roughly chopped*
- [ ] *1/4 cup cilantro, packed*
- [ ] *1 teaspoon fish sauce*
- [ ] *1 tablespoon jalapeño pepper, diced small*
- [ ] *6 tablespoons vegetable oil*
- [ ] *Black pepper, freshly ground*
- [ ] *Kosher salt*

Directions:

1. Preheat the oven to450F.

2. Clean and remove the stems from the mushrooms.

3. With the gill-side down, put the mushrooms on a foil-lined baking sheet. Brush them with the melted ghee. Roast for about 12 minutes. Flip the mushrooms over and roast for about 5–10 minutes more or until the mushroom liquid has evaporated.

4. While the mushrooms are roasting, de-vein and remove the tails of the shrimp. Chop them into medium-sized pieces.

5. In the work bowl of a food processor, toss the shrimp with the bacon, cilantro, scallions, jalapeño pepper, vegetable oil, and fish sauce; season with the salt and pepper. Process the ingredients until it turns into a coarsely chopped texture with a pasty, sticky, chunky mixture.

6. With a small dish or spoon, scoop out the filling and fill each mushroom with the paste.

7. Return the mushroom to the oven; cook for about 8-10 minutes or until the mixture is set. Serve topped with Sriracha if desired.

Grilled Calamari & Roasted Peppers

This super easy and quick to flash-grilled calamari dinner meal is a great seafood dish. A tangy salad is a perfect complement to this recipe.

Prep Time: 30 minutes; **Cook Time:** 10 minutes

Serving Size: 257 g; **Serves:** 3; **Calories:** 451

Total Fat: 35.2 g **Saturated Fat:** 8.9 g; **Trans Fat:** 0 g

Protein: 24.3 g; **Net Carbs:** 7.7 g

Total Carbs: 8.8 g; **Dietary Fibre:** 1.1 g; **Sugars:** 2 g

Cholesterol: 366 mg; **Sodium**: 146 mg; **Potassium**: 526 mg;

Ingredients:

- ☐ *1 pound squid, cleaned, gutted*
- ☐ *1 medium red bell pepper*
- ☐ *2 small shallot, thinly sliced*
- ☐ *2 tablespoon balsamic vinegar*
- ☐ *2 tablespoon lemon juice, from 1 lemon*
- ☐ *1/4 cup Italian parsley leaves*
- ☐ *3 tablespoons bacon grease, melted or your fat of choice*
- ☐ *4 tablespoons olive oil, extra virgin*
- ☐ *Black pepper, freshly ground*
- ☐ *Kosher salt*

Directions:

1. Place the bell pepper directly on your gas range. Turn on the heat and char it until the skin is black all over. Place the pepper in a bowl. Tightly cover with plastic wrap or foil. Let them steam for at least 15 minutes. Rub off the blackened skin. Remove the stems, seeds, and the ribs. Cut into strips. Set aside.

2. Gut the squids, rinse, and dry. Cut each one open so they would lie flat on the grill. Remove the skin if you desire.

3. Toss the squid with the bacon grease; season with salt and pepper to taste.

4. In a small mixing bowl, combine the balsamic vinegar and the shallots. Allow to mellow out.

5. Preheat the grill on high. When the grill is hot, cook the squid for about 20–30 seconds per side. The tentacles will take longer to cook. However, don't cook them for too long or they will turn to rubber.

6. When the squid is flash-grilled, slice it. Put in a bowl. Add the lemon juice and pour in the olive oil. Toss to coat evenly. Transfer to the balsamic-shallot mix. Add the sliced pepper; season with salt and pepper. Mix everything well. Sprinkle with parsley.

7. Taste and adjust lemon juice, salt, and pepper according to taste.

Edamame Pesto Zoodle and Cabbage Salad

This dish is very high in vitamin C and low in cholesterol. The green soybeans make this recipe a delicious mix of healthy carbs, fiber, and protein.

Prep Time: 15 minutes; **Cook Time:** 5 minutes

Serving Size: 175 g; **Serves:** 4; **Calories:** 273

Total Fat: 23.2 g **Saturated Fat:** 5.6 g; **Trans Fat:** 0 g

Protein: 9.4 g; **Net Carbs:** 6.6 g

Total Carbs: 10.4 g; **Dietary Fibre:** 3.8 g; **Sugars:** 3.1 g

Cholesterol: 17 mg; **Sodium:** 350 mg; **Potassium:** 512 mg;

Vitamin A: 22%; **Vitamin C:** 69%; **Calcium:** 20%; **Iron:** 13%

Ingredients:

- ☐ *8 ounces zoodles (zucchini noodles)*
- ☐ *2 tablespoons vegetable oil*
- ☐ *1 1/2 cups thinly sliced red cabbage (from 1/4 small head)*
- ☐ *1/2 cup (2 ounces) crumbled feta*

For the pesto:

- ☐ *1/2 cup fresh cilantro leaves*
- ☐ *1/2 cup fresh parsley leaves*
- ☐ *1/4 cup whole raw almonds*

- ☐ *1 small clove garlic*
- ☐ *1/2 cup shelled frozen edamame, defrosted*
- ☐ *1/4 teaspoon red pepper flakes*
- ☐ *1/4 teaspoon coarse salt*
- ☐ *2 tablespoons lime juice*
- ☐ *2 tablespoons olive oil*
- ☐ *1 tablespoon water*

Directions:

1. To make the pesto, place parsley, cilantro, garlic, edamame, almonds, salt, and pepper flakes in a food processor; pulse for about 30 seconds or until incorporated. With the motor running, drizzle in the oil, juice, and water; process for another 30 seconds until the mixture is smooth. By tablespoons, add more water if necessary. Transfer to a large bowl.

2. Add the vegetable oil over low to medium heat in a large pan. Add the zoodles; sauté for a couple of minutes, stirring gently until soft. Add to the bowl with pesto. Add the cabbage; toss everything until well-coated with the pesto.

3. Divide the zoodle salad into 4 serving plates; sprinkle with the feta cheese.

Orange Dijon Chicken

This chicken recipe makes a delicious bang using just a few ingredients. This home-made version of a restaurant-quality Dijon mustard marinade makes for a zesty, sweet dish that's a hit for both kids and kids at heart.

Prep Time: 5 minutes, plus marinating; **Cook Time:** 40 minutes

Serving Size: 414 g; **Serves:** 4; **Calories:** 629

Total Fat: 22.3 g **Saturated Fat:** 5.5 g; **Trans Fat:** 0 g

Protein: 96.1 g; **Net Carbs:** 3.9 g

Total Carbs: 5.9 g; **Dietary Fibre:** 2 g; **Sugars:** 1.7 g

Cholesterol: 299 mg; **Sodium:** 1969 mg; **Potassium:** 816 mg;

Vitamin A: 6%; **Vitamin C:** 26%; **Calcium:** 8%; **Iron:** 32%

Ingredients:

- ☐ *3 pounds chicken thighs or drumsticks*
- ☐ *Italian parsley or chives, minced*

For the marinade:

- ☐ *1/4 cup orange juice, freshly squeezed*
- ☐ *3/4 cup Dijon mustard*
- ☐ *2 tablespoons avocado oil or extra virgin olive oil*
- ☐ *6 garlic cloves, minced*
- ☐ *2 teaspoons kosher salt*

Directions:

1. Preheat the oven to 425F or 400F for convection. Place the rack in the middle position. Line a rimmed baking sheet with aluminum foil. Place a stainless steel wire rack on top.

2. In a large mixing bowl, combine all the marinade ingredients together, adjusting the amount of salt according to taste. Mix well.

3. Put the chicken into the marinade. Coat each piece well. If desired, marinade in the morning for dinner cooking. Don't marinade for more than a day.

4. Gently shake off excess marinade from the chicken. In a single layer, lay the drumsticks on the wire rack on the prepared baking sheet.

5. Roast for about 20 minutes. Flip the drumsticks over and rotate the tray 180 degrees. Continue roasting for 20 minutes more or until the meat is cooked to the internal temperature of 170F and the skin is browned. Serve with a sprinkle of parsley.

Portuguese Green Soup

This Portuguese recipe is a hearty, creamy soup with the wonderful tastes of collard greens, potatoes, and chorizo. Leftovers become creamier the next day. If you don't like a thicker consistency, just add some water to thin your soup. You can also use kale instead of collard greens for a more bitter taste.

Prep Time: 20 minutes **Cook Time:** 30 minutes

Serving Size: 480 g; **Serves:** 6; **Calories:** 225

Total Fat: 18.7 g **Saturated Fat**: 3.6 g; **Trans Fat**: 0 g

Protein: 2.8 g; **Net Carbs:** 6.6 g

Total Carbs: 14.1 g; **Dietary Fibre:** 4.1 g; **Sugars:** 1.4 g

Cholesterol: 0 mg; **Sodium:** 26 mg; **Potassium:** 239 mg;

Vitamin A: 50%; **Vitamin C**: 57%; **Calcium:** 10%; **Iron:** 2%

Ingredients:

- ☐ *8 tablespoons vegetable oil*
- ☐ *1 cup chopped onion*
- ☐ *2 teaspoons chopped garlic*
- ☐ *2 cups potatoes peeled and cut into chunks (okay in this keto soup)*
- ☐ *2 quarts water*
- ☐ *Carcass of one left over Chicken, with skin and fat*
- ☐ *Salt and black pepper*
- ☐ *1-pound collard greens or kale, washed, trimmed and sliced into 1-inch strips*

Directions:

1. In a soup pot, heat the vegetable oil, add the onions and garlic and cook for 3–5 minutes until the onions are translucent.

2. Add water and chicken. Cook for about 10 minutes. Cool and separate meat, from bones and fat.

3. Cook the potatoes in the pot of water for 20 minutes. When the potatoes are tender, mash them lightly right in the pot.

4. Add the chicken meat, skin, and fat to the potatoes. Cook until the soup is boiling.

5. Add the collard greens (or kale).

6. Boil veggies for only 5 minutes.

Beef Salpicao

The time to marinade the meat may take quite a while, but the preparation is simple and only takes 10 minutes to cook. I love to add large red onions that are cut into rings when the recipe is cooked and cook for a few additional minutes until the onions are translucent.

Prep Time: 40 minutes **Cook Time:** 10 minutes

Serving Size: 173 g; **Serves:** 4; **Calories:** 525

Total Fat: 40 g **Saturated Fat:** 12.3 g; **Trans Fat:** 0 g

Protein: 33.4 g; **Net Carbs:** 6.2 g

Total Carbs: 6.2 g; **Dietary Fibre:** 0 g; **Sugars:** 3.8 g

Cholesterol: 120 mg; **Sodium:** 951 mg; **Potassium:** 436 mg;

Vitamin A: 4%; **Vitamin C:** 3%; **Calcium:** 3%; **Iron:** 13%

Ingredients:

☐ *1 pounds beef tenderloin or sirloin; cut into cubes*

- [ ] *1 teaspoon salt*
- [ ] *1/2 teaspoon ground black pepper*
- [ ] *2 tablespoons butter*
- [ ] *2 tablespoons oyster sauce*
- [ ] *3 tablespoons garlic, minced*
- [ ] *7 tablespoons vegetable oil*
- [ ] *5 tablespoons Worcestershire Sauce*

Directions:

1. In a bowl, combine the beef, garlic, salt, and pepper until well mixed. Allow to stand for 10 minutes.

2. After 10 minutes, add in the olive oil. Marinade for at least 30 minutes.

3. Heat a skillet or a pan. Once the pan is hot enough, put the beef. Sear the meat until the outer part turns brown. Toss the meat while searing so that all the sides are cooked.

4. Add the oyster sauce and then the Worcestershire sauce. Continue tossing until the liquid dries up.

5. Add in the butter. Cook for about 2-3 minutes more. Serve hot over favorite vegetables or leaves.

Feta Cheesy Pesto Chicken with Olives

This dish combines the best from Greece and Italy, feta cheese, and pesto, to make a meal that is loved by both old and young. It's deliciously creamy with all the goodness of a low carb ketogenic meal packed with vitamins and minerals.

Prep Time: 15-20 minutes **Cook Time:** 20-30 minutes

Serving Size: 352 g; **Serves:** 4; **Calories:** 869

Total Fat: 67.2 g **Saturated Fat:** 33 g; **Trans Fat:** 0 g

Protein: 59 g; **Net Carbs:** 5.4 g

Total Carbs: 6.9 g; **Dietary Fibre:** 1.5 g; **Sugars:** 2.6 g

Cholesterol: 281 mg; **Sodium:** 1017 mg; **Potassium:** 480 mg;

Vitamin A: 95%; **Vitamin C:** 29%; **Calcium:** 41%; **Iron:** 15%

Ingredients:

- ☐ *1 1/2 pounds (700 g) chicken, breast or thighs*
- ☐ *4 ounce (100 g) green or red pesto*
- ☐ *1/2 pound (225 g) feta cheese; dice*
- ☐ *1/2 cup (120 ml) pitted olives, green or black*
- ☐ *1 garlic clove; chop finely*
- ☐ *1 1/2 cups (400 ml) heavy whipping cream*
- ☐ *Salt and pepper*
- ☐ *5 tablespoons butter*
- ☐ *5 tablespoons olive oil*

Directions:

1. Preheat the oven to 400F (200C).

2. Cut the chicken breasts or thighs into pieces; season with salt and pepper. Melt butter with the olive oil in a pan. Add the chicken. Fry until the meat is golden brown.

3. In a bowl, mix the heavy cream, the pesto, and the grease in the pan.

4. Put the chicken into a baking dish. Add in the olives, feta cheese, and garlic. Pour the pesto mix over. Bake for about 20-30 minutes or until the dish turns into a nice color.

5. Serve with baby spinach and other leafy greens you prefer. Toss with a generous amount of olive oil and a little salt.

Goat Cheese and Garlic-Stuffed Roasted Chicken Breast

Stuffing chicken may sound a little tedious and fussy, but the effort is worth it. This version is very easy, and you'll only need a few ingredients. The skin comes out crisp and cheese permeates every bite with a garlicky aroma and a hint of lemon.

Prep Time: 20 minutes **Cook Time:** 30 minutes

Serving Size: 205 g; **Serves:** 4; **Calories:** 647

Total Fat: 49.9 g **Saturated Fat:** 13.2 g; **Trans Fat:** 0 g

Protein: 46.8 g; **Net Carbs:** 1.3 g

Total Carbs: 1.3 g; **Dietary Fibre:** 0 g; **Sugars:** 0.5 g

Cholesterol: 145 mg; **Sodium:** 176 mg; **Potassium:** 385 mg;

Vitamin A: 9%; **Vitamin C:** 9%; **Calcium:** 15%; **Iron:** 12%

Ingredients:

- [ ] *4 medium chicken breast halves, skin-on and bone-in*
- [ ] *2 ounces soft goat cheese*
- [ ] *2 stalks fresh, green garlic (or 1 tablespoon chives plus 2 cloves regular garlic)*
- [ ] *1/2 lemon; zest and juice (about 1 tablespoon juice and 1/2 teaspoon zest)*
- [ ] *1 tablespoon Italian parsley, finely chopped*
- [ ] *Salt and freshly ground black pepper*
- [ ] *10 tablespoons vegetable oil*

Directions:

1. Preheat the oven to 425F.

2. In a bowl, mix the goat cheese, lemon juice, lemon zest, and parsley until well combined.

3. Slice the garlic bulbs very thinly. Chop about 1/3 of the green stalks. If using chives and regular garlic, mince finely. Add the garlic into the goat cheese mix; lightly season with a pinch of salt and pepper.

4. Run your fingers underneath the chicken skin to loosen it, making sure to leave it attached at the edges. Cut a deep slit into the chicken breast, about 3 inches long and 1 1/2 inch deep. Divide the goat cheese mix into four portions. Stuff 1/4 of the goat cheese mix into the slit of one chicken breast, pushing it as deep as possible. If necessary, use a toothpick to hold the slit close. Stuff another 1/4 of the goat cheese mix under the skin of the chicken breast, sliding your finger across the top of the skin to spread the cheese in an even layer. Repeat the process for the other chicken breast.

5. Place the chicken breast on a lined baking sheet or a baking dish. Drizzle the oil over the breasts. Bake for about 30 minutes or until the skin is crisp is brown, crisp, and an instant read thermometer reads 165F when inserted into the thickest part. Immediately serve with vegetables or green salad.

Spicy-Choco Mushroom Beef

This warm dinner is filling and hearty. The chocolate adds depth to the flavor of the dish. Sometimes, I tweak this version a bit by adding 1/2 cup black coffee, 1 large bay leaf, a bit of fresh ground nutmeg, and 1 tablespoon of Worcestershire sauce.

Prep Time: 10 minutes **Cook Time:** 40 minutes	
Serving Size: 222 g; **Serves:** 5; **Calories:** 437	
Total Fat: 34.7 g **Saturated Fat**: 8 g; **Trans Fat**: 0 g	
Protein: 24.7 g; **Net Carbs:** 6.3 g	
Total Carbs: 9.2 g; **Dietary Fibre:** 2.9 g; **Sugars:** 2.6 g	
Cholesterol: 66mg; **Sodium:** 495 mg; **Potassium:** 612 mg;	
Vitamin A: 39%; **Vitamin C**: 15%; **Calcium:** 4%; **Iron:** 83%	

Ingredients:

- [ ] *1 pound ground beef*
- [ ] *1 cup mushrooms, chopped*
- [ ] *4 bacon slices*
- [ ] *2 tablespoons cocoa powder, unsweetened*
- [ ] *2 teaspoons dried oregano*
- [ ] *2 tablespoons ketchup, no sugar added*
- [ ] *2 tablespoons chili powder*
- [ ] *10 ounces canned tomatoes with green chilies*
- [ ] *1/2 onion, chopped*
- [ ] *1/2 cup water*
- [ ] *1 teaspoon beef bouillon concentrate*
- [ ] *1 tablespoon smoked paprika*

☐ *10 tablespoons vegetable oil, divided*

Directions:

1. Put a big, heavy skillet over medium heat. Fry the bacon until crisp.

2. Remove from the skillet. Transfer to the plate. Set aside.

3. In the same skillet, add the oil. Put in the ground beef. Brown and crumble. After a few minutes of putting the beef into the skillet, put in the onion and the mushrooms.

4. When the beef was browned. Add the rest of the ingredients. Stir it well. Adjust the burner to low. Simmer for about 20 minutes. Serve topped with crumbled bacon. If desired, add avocado, shredded cheddar, and sour cream.

Chicken Nacho Casserole

Ketogenic dishes and casserole go hand in hand when making high-fat, low-carb dishes. You will be able to use all the cheese you want to create ooey-gooey meals everyone will enjoy. The chili seasoning gives the dish kick, the balance of sweetness and acidity of the tomatoes has a well-balanced taste, and there's all the cheese you wanted. The cauliflower lightens this dish and adds fluffy goodness to every bite.

Prep Time: 20 minutes **Cook Time:** 30 minutes

Serving Size: 267 g; **Serves:** 6; **Calories:** 517

Total Fat: 40.3 g **Saturated Fat**: 15.5 g; **Trans Fat:** 0 g

Protein: 32.5 g; **Net Carbs:** 5.3 g

Total Carbs: 7.3 g; **Dietary Fibre:** 2 g; **Sugars:** 2 g

Cholesterol: 117 mg; **Sodium**: 512 mg; **Potassium**: 516 mg;

Vitamin A: 16%; **Vitamin C**: 64%; **Calcium**: 26%; **Iron**: 10%

Ingredients:

- [ ] *4 ounces cream cheese*
- [ ] *4 ounces cheddar cheese*
- [ ] *3 tablespoons Parmesan cheese*
- [ ] *2 tablespoons olive oil*
- [ ] *1/4 cup sour cream*
- [ ] *1 package (16 ounces) frozen cauliflower*
- [ ] *1 medium jalapeño pepper*
- [ ] *1 cup tomatoes with green chilies*
- [ ] *1 3/4 pounds chicken thighs, skinless, boneless*
- [ ] *1 1/2 teaspoons chili seasoning*
- [ ] *Salt and pepper, to taste*

Directions:

1. Preheat the oven to 375F. Chop the chicken into bite-size pieces. Season with the salt, pepper, and chili seasoning.

2. In a skillet over medium-high heat, cook the chicken until all sides are browned.

3. Add the cream cheese, sour cream, and 3/4 of the cheddar cheese into the chicken. Stir together until mixed and the cheese is melted. Add the tomatoes with the green chilies. Mix well.

4. Pour the chicken mixture into a casserole.

5. Microwave the cauliflower until cooked through. Put into a mixing bowl. Add in the remaining cheese. With an immersion blender, blend until mash potato in texture. Season with salt and pepper to taste.

6. Cut the jalapeño into chunks.

7. Spread the cauliflower mixture over the chicken mixture. Sprinkle with the jalapeño chunks. Bake for 15-20 minutes until the jalapeños are cooked and the casserole top has some color. Slice and then serve. If desired, chop with cilantro.

Flank Steak Roulade

The best part about this recipe is that you can make the roulade several days ahead of time and then cook when you want to enjoy a fancy meal. Prepare it on a lazy Sunday and you'll have a meal that you can pop into the oven during a busy weeknight.

Prep Time: 30 minutes **Cook Time:** 20 minutes

Serving Size: 236 g; **Serves:** 6; **Calories:** 522

Total Fat: 40.7 g **Saturated Fat:** 12.1 g; **Trans Fat:** 0 g

Protein: 34.8 g; **Net Carbs:** 2.2 g

Total Carbs: 3.9 g; **Dietary Fibre:** 1.7 g; **Sugars:** 1.4 g

Cholesterol: 78 mg; **Sodium:** 586 mg; **Potassium:** 726 mg;

Vitamin A: 89%; **Vitamin C:** 66%; **Calcium:** 6%; **Iron:** 19%

Ingredients:

- ☐ *1 1/2 pounds flank steak*
- ☐ *4 thick slices bacon, diced*
- ☐ *1/2 pound baby spinach*
- ☐ *1 small green zucchini, diced*
- ☐ *2 tablespoons ghee or coconut oil*
- ☐ *1/4 cup water*
- ☐ *1 teaspoon kosher salt, divided*
- ☐ *1 teaspoon chili powder*
- ☐ *1 teaspoon black pepper, divided*
- ☐ *1 medium red pepper, diced*
- ☐ *1 garlic clove, pressed*
- ☐ *11 tablespoons vegetable oil*

Directions:

1. Preheat the oven to 400F.

2. Over high heat, heat a large sauté pan until very hot. Put the spinach and the water. Cover the pan. Allow the spinach to steam for about 2 minutes undisturbed. Uncover. Allow the spinach to cool. Drain excess water and press out the water from the spinach.

3. With the fibers parallel to your stabilizing hand, butterfly the steak, carefully not slicing it into 2 pieces. Season the inside part of the meat with about 1/4 teaspoon salt and1/4 teaspoon pepper to taste.

4. Over medium heat, heat a sauté pan. Put the bacon and cook for about 3–4 minutes. Add the vegetable oil, zucchini, and the peppers. Continue cooking for 3–4 minutes more. Sprinkle with the chili powder, 1/2 teaspoon salt, and 1/2 teaspoon pepper. Mix well. Continue cooking until the vegetables are tender. Remove the pan from the heat and allow to cool.

5. Evenly spread the cooled bacon-vegetable mixture over the steak. Roll the flank steak. Tie with a butcher twine. Season the outside with the remaining salt and pepper. Freeze for up to 3 days or cook immediately. If freezing, allow to thaw at room temperature.

6. Over high heat, heat a large sauté pan. Put in the ghee or the coconut oil until smoking hot. Sear all sides of the roulade until golden brown.

7. Transfer the roulade to the oven; cook for about 18–20 minutes or until the internal temperature is 120F for medium rare.

8. Remove from the oven and allow to rest for about 20 minutes. Slice and remove the twine. Serve.

Fiery Chicken Wings Barbecue

These extremely great tasting chicken wings are easy to make and healthy. Plus, by cooking this version, you won't need to get messy frying the chicken wings. The marinade makes this deliciously spicy meal.

Prep Time: 10 minutes **Cook Time:** 40 minutes

Serving Size: 197g; **Serves:** 6; **Calories:** 464

Total Fat: 29.7 g **Saturated Fat:** 18.9 g; **Trans Fat:** 0 g

Protein: 44.1 g; **Net Carbs:** 3.2 g

Total Carbs: 4 g; **Dietary Fibre:** 0.8 g; **Sugars:** 2.3 g

Cholesterol: 135 mg; **Sodium:** 180 mg; **Potassium:** 453 mg;

Vitamin A: 16%; **Vitamin C:** 3%; **Calcium:** 4%; **Iron:** 12%

Ingredients:

- ☐ *2 pounds chicken wings*
- ☐ *4-6 celery stalks, for serving*

☐ *Sea salt*

For the barbecue sauce:

☐ *2 garlic cloves*

☐ *1 teaspoon smoked paprika*

☐ *1 teaspoon cayenne pepper*

☐ *1 tablespoon maple syrup*

☐ *1 tablespoon ancho chili powder*

☐ *1/2 cup coconut oil*

☐ *1/4 cup red wine vinegar*

Directions:

1. Preheat the oven to 375F.

2. Line a sheet pan with parchment paper.

3. Put all of the barbecue sauce ingredients into a blender. Blend until the texture is smooth; season with salt to taste.

4. Put the chicken and the sauce into a large bowl. Toss to coat the meat. Spread the coated chicken into the sheet pan. Roast uncovered for about 40 minutes or until cooked through.

5. Allow to cool for at least 10 minutes. Serve with celery sticks.

Cauliflower Rice Vegetable Sauté

The original dish uses cooked brown rice. This version uses cauliflower rice, making it low carb.

Prep Time: 20 minutes **Cook Time:** 20 minutes	
Serving Size: 191 g; **Serves:** 4; **Calories:** 245	
Total Fat: 20 g **Saturated Fat**: 4.4 g; **Trans Fat**: 0 g	
Protein: 9.4 g; **Net Carbs:** 7 g	
Total Carbs: 10.5 g; **Dietary Fibre:** 3.5 g; **Sugars:** 3.7 g	
Cholesterol: 8 mg; **Sodium:** 488 mg; **Potassium:** 480mg;	
Vitamin A: 8%; **Vitamin C:** 94%; **Calcium:** 14%; **Iron**: 15%	

Ingredients:

For the cauliflower rice:

- ☐ *1 cup cauliflower rice*
- ☐ *2 tablespoons vegetable oil*
- ☐ *2 grams chicken bouillon (1/2 of a cube)*
- ☐ *Salt and pepper, to taste*

For the vegetables:

- ☐ *2 tablespoons vegetable oil*
- ☐ *1 cup onion (about 1 large), chopped*
- ☐ *2 cups small broccoli florets*
- ☐ *1 package (8-ounce) sliced mushrooms*

- [ ] *1 teaspoon dried thyme*

- [ ] *1/2 teaspoon salt*

- [ ] *1/2 teaspoon minced garlic*

- [ ] *1/4 teaspoon pepper*

- [ ] *1/2 cup (2 ounces) mozzarella cheese, part-skim, shredded*

- [ ] *3 tablespoons chopped walnuts, toasted*

Directions:

1. In a large-sized, nonstick skillet, heat the oil over medium-high heat. Add the onion and sauté for 5 minutes. Add the broccoli and cover. Adjust the heat to low and cook for 3 minutes. Uncover and add the mushrooms, thyme, salt, garlic, and pepper; sauté for 5 minutes or until the mushrooms are soft.

2. Heat the oil in a sauté pan. Add the cauliflower rice. Crumble the bouillon over the rice; stir-fry to cook until soft and seasoning with salt and pepper to taste.

3. Divide the cauliflower rice between 4 large serving bowls. Divide the vegetable mix over the cauliflower rice. Evenly divide and sprinkle the cheese and the walnuts between each serving.

Keto-lasagna

If cauliflower is the low-carb substitute for rice, then spaghetti squash is the low-carb substitute for pasta. This recipe is easy to layer up and makes for a super hearty dinner meal

Prep Time: 20 minutes **Cook Time:** 40 minutes

Serving Size: 308 g; **Serves:** 8; **Calories:** 706

Total Fat: 55.5 g **Saturated Fat:** 23.4 g; **Trans Fat:** 0 g

Protein: 40.4 g; **Net Carbs:** 9.6 g

Total Carbs: 10.6 g; **Dietary Fibre:** 1 g; **Sugars:** 2.9 g

Cholesterol: 141 mg; **Sodium:** 1592 mg; **Potassium:** 528 mg;

Vitamin A: 21%; **Vitamin C:** 10%; **Calcium:** 62%; **Iron:** 12%

Ingredients:

- ☐ *4 cups spaghetti squash*
- ☐ *4 ounces of cream cheese*
- ☐ *1/4 cup of full-fat ricotta cheese*
- ☐ *16 ounces of shredded mozzarella*
- ☐ *6 ounces of shredded blended cheese*
- ☐ *bag of pepperoni slices*

For marinara sauce:

- ☐ *1 lb. of cooked Italian sausage*
- ☐ *2 cans of tomato sauce*
- ☐ *4 tablespoons olive oil*
- ☐ *clove of Garlic*

- □ *1 small onion*
- □ *1/3 cup red wine*

Directions:

1. Use homemade or pre-made tomato sauce (be careful of the sugar content).

2. Stir in cooked and crumbled Italian sausage.

3. Cook spaghetti squash (microwave for quickest results).

4. First, layer the tomato sauce in a 914 pan.

5. Next, put one layer of the cooked spaghetti squash over the sauce.

6. Put the marina sauce with sausage over the top of the squash.

7. Add a layer of shredded mozzarella.

8. Next, add the cream cheese and ricotta cheese.

9. Another layer of spaghetti squash.

10. Add the rest of the sausage marinara.

11. Add another layer of mozzarella.

12. A sprinkle of shredded blended cheese.

13. Place pepperoni slices on top.

14. Bake Keto Sagna at 350 degrees for about 35-40 minutes.

Spaghetti Squash with Meat Sauce

Not only is spaghetti squash a great low carb alternative to spaghetti, but it also makes your dishes gluten-free. When cooked, the squash flesh shreds into thin threadlike pieces similar to normal spaghetti or vermicelli. This low-carb version is tasty and super filling. You can substitute for turkey or chicken and add herbs like oregano, parsley, and fennel for more flavor.

Prep Time: 10 minutes **Cook Time:** 1 hour

Serving Size: 413 g; **Serves:** 8; **Calories:** 343

Total Fat: 20.8 g **Saturated Fat:** 5.8 g; **Trans Fat:** 0 g

Protein: 20 g; **Net Carbs:** 21.1 g

Total Carbs: 22.8 g; **Dietary Fibre:** 1.7 g; **Sugars:** 5 g

Cholesterol: 44 mg; **Sodium:** 795 mg; **Potassium:** 752 mg;

Vitamin A: 12%; **Vitamin C:** 22%; **Calcium:** 20%; **Iron:** 34%

Ingredients:

- ☐ *1 spaghetti squash (about 4 pounds)*
- ☐ *32 ounces tomato sauce*
- ☐ *1 tablespoon minced garlic*
- ☐ *1 tablespoon Italian seasoning*
- ☐ *Parmesan cheese to taste*
- ☐ *3/4 lb. ground beef, pork or turkey*
- ☐ *8 tablespoon vegetable oil*

Directions:

1. Cut Spaghetti Squash in half and scrape out the inside.

2. Place face down in a glass container and add water until it goes over the cut portion.

3. Cook at 375 degrees for 45 minutes or until soft when forked.

4. While the spaghetti squash is cooking, brown meat with the vegetable oil.

5. Add seasoning and mix.

6. Add spaghetti sauce.

7. Carefully remove spaghetti squash from the oven and use a fork to create the spaghetti.

8. Serve the Spaghetti Squash with the sauce and garnish with Parmesan Cheese.

Sea Scallops Curry

Scallops are high in protein and low in fat. They also make a fast, delicious meal.

Prep Time: 10 minutes **Cook Time:** 10 minutes

Serving Size: 240 g; **Serves:** 4; **Calories:** 455

Total Fat: 37.4 g **Saturated Fat:** 7.6 g; **Trans Fat:** 0 g

Protein: 25.2 g; **Net Carbs:** 4.8 g

Total Carbs: 4.8 g; **Dietary Fibre:** 0 g; **Sugars:** 0 g

Cholesterol: 52 mg; **Sodium:** 654 mg; **Potassium:** 539 mg;

Vitamin A: 6%; **Vitamin C:** 14%; **Calcium:** 6%; **Iron:** 5%

Ingredients:

- ☐ *1 1/2 teaspoons fresh lemon juice*
- ☐ *1 1/4 pounds sea scallops*
- ☐ *1/2 teaspoon salt*
- ☐ *1/4 cup half-and-half*
- ☐ *1/4 teaspoon pepper*
- ☐ *2 tablespoons chopped fresh parsley*
- ☐ *2 tablespoons olive oil, divided*
- ☐ *2 tablespoons thinly sliced green onions*
- ☐ *2/3 cup chicken broth*
- ☐ *3/4 teaspoon curry powder*
- ☐ *4 teaspoons almond flour*

☐ *8 tablespoons vegetable oil*

Directions:

1. Combine the broth, half-and-half, lemon juice, curry powder, salt, and pepper; stir well and set aside.

2. Pat the scallops dry with paper towels to remove excess moisture; lightly coat with the flour.

3. Add the oil in a nonstick skillet. Place the pan over medium-high heat and heat the oil until hot. Add half of the scallops; cook each side for 2 minutes, remove from the pan, and set aside. Repeat the process with the remaining scallops. Return the first set of cooked scallops in the pan. Add the broth mixture; bring to a boil.

4. Cook the mixture for 3 minutes more or until the sauce is slightly thick. Transfer to a deep serving dish. Sprinkle with green onions and parsley; serve.

Rosemary Butter Chicken

This entry is simple but elegant. It takes a little effort to prepare, too!

Prep Time: 10 minutes **Cook Time:** 25 minutes

Serving Size: 183 g; **Serves:** 4; **Calories:** 486

Total Fat: 35.8 g **Saturated Fat:** 15.1 g; **Trans Fat:** 0 g

Protein: 33.3 g; **Net Carbs:** 1.8 g

Total Carbs: 1.8 g; **Dietary Fibre:** 0 g; **Sugars:** 0 g

Cholesterol: 152 mg; **Sodium:** 187 mg; **Potassium:** 327 mg;

Vitamin A: 13%; **Vitamin C:** 1%; **Calcium:** 4%; **Iron:** 10%

Ingredients:

☐ *4 boneless skinless chicken breast halves (4 ounces each)*

☐ *4 tablespoons butter, divided*

☐ *3 tablespoons vegetable oil*

☐ *1/2 cup white wine or chicken broth*

☐ *1/2 cup heavy whipping cream*

☐ *1 tablespoon minced fresh rosemary*

Directions:

1. In a large skillet, melt 1 tablespoon of the butter with the vegetable oil over medium heat. Add the chickens; cook each side for about 4 to 5 minutes or until a meat thermometer reads 165F. Remove from the skillet and

keep warm.

2. Add the wine to the skillet; cook over medium-ow heat, stirring to loosen the browned bits. Add the cream; bring to a boil. Reduce the heat; cook, stirring, until slightly thick. Stir in the rosemary and the remaining butter until well blended. Pour the sauce over the chicken.

Notes:

This dish is perfect with full-bodied white wine, such as Viognier or Chardonnay.

Spicy Chocolate BBQ Sauce

This version still has the same classic taste that most people love in most popular sauces – tart, sweet, and slightly sweet, but with a seductive chocolate twist. This sweet and spicy, smooth barbecue sauce is made richer with the addition of chocolate. If you like your sauces hotter, just add more chili powder. For use with the recipe bellow.

Prep Time: 5 minutes **Cook Time:** until bubbling

Serving Size: 111 g; **Serves:** 4; **Calories:** 282

Total Fat: 23.9 g **Saturated Fat**: 14.9 g; **Trans Fat**: 0 g

Protein: 3.1 g; **Net Carbs:** 21.1 g

Total Carbs: 18.6 g; **Dietary Fibre:** 1.8 g; **Sugars:** 14.1 g

Cholesterol: 61 mg; **Sodium**: 1583 mg; **Potassium**: 345 mg;

Vitamin A: 40%; **Vitamin C**: 18%; **Calcium**: 3%; **Iron**: 7%

Ingredients:

- ☐ *1 cup ketchup*
- ☐ *2 cloves garlic, crushed*
- ☐ *8 tablespoons butter*
- ☐ *2 teaspoons paprika (regular or smoked)*
- ☐ *1 tsp chili powder*
- ☐ *2 tablespoons cocoa powder, unsweetened*
- ☐ *½ teaspoon smoked salt or pink Himalayan rock salt*
- ☐ *2 Tablespoons apple cider vinegar*
- ☐ *2 Tablespoons coconut amino*
- ☐ *2 Tablespoons Erythritol*
- ☐ *Freshly ground black pepper*

Directions:

1. Place everything into a saucepan and heat over medium until bubbling. Use with BBQ meats.

2. You can transfer BBQ sauce to a glass jar and keep up to a month in the refrigerator.

BBQ Pork Ribs

This dish will require some time to prepare and the right technique to grill, but it is well worth the effort. Follow the instructions to the dot and you will have a smoked baby back ribs with plenty of flavors. This is finger licking good!

Prep Time: 15 minutes, plus overnight marinating **Cook Time:** 60 minutes

Serving Size: 546 g; **Serves:** 4; **Calories:** 1493

Total Fat: 106.2 g **Saturated Fat:** 32.3 g; **Trans Fat:** 0 g

Protein: 121.5 g; **Net Carbs:** 5.9 g

Total Carbs: 8.2 g; **Dietary Fibre:** 2.3 g; **Sugars:** 2.6 g

Cholesterol: 467 mg; **Sodium:** 1444 mg; **Potassium:** 1474 mg;

Vitamin A: 20%; **Vitamin C:** 11%; **Calcium:** 19%; **Iron:** 42%

Ingredients:

☐ *2 average racks pork ribs (about 2 pounds each)*

For the marinade:

- [ ] *2 medium white onion*
- [ ] *4cloves garlic*
- [ ] *2 teaspoon cumin*
- [ ] *2 teaspoon paprika*
- [ ] *2 teaspoon chili powder*
- [ ] *1/2 cup olive oil*
- [ ] *2 teaspoon salt (smoked works best)*
- [ ] *1 teaspoon freshly ground pepper*

Directions:

1. Prepare the marinade by placing all ingredients (except meat) in a blender and pulsing until smooth.

2. Cover ribs with the marinade and place in fridge overnight.

3. Preheat oven to medium-low (about 300 degrees F.).

4. Place ribs in the oven and cook slowly for 60 minutes.

5. Heat grill.

6. Place cooked ribs on the grill and finish cooking for about 15 minutes.

7. Serve with Spicy Chocolate BBQ Sauce or any BBQ sauce that you love.

Meat Loaf Bacon Wrap

This is probably the best low-carb meatloaf. The meaty goodness of this dish is mouth-watering. Covered with bacon, the loaf comes out juicy and moist! If you have kids, this is also a great way to hide their vegetables. Perfect served with low-carb green beans and mashed cauliflower.

Prep Time: 30 minutes **Cook Time:** 90 minutes

Serving Size: 173 g; **Serves:** 8; **Calories:** 466

Total Fat: 36.2 g **Saturated Fat:** 8.4 g; **Trans Fat:** 0 g

Protein: 30.5 g; **Net Carbs:** 4.1 g

Total Carbs: 4.7 g; **Dietary Fibre:** 0.6 g; **Sugars:** 3.3 g

Cholesterol: 104 mg; **Sodium:** 1007 mg; **Potassium:** 519 mg;

Vitamin A: 6%; **Vitamin C:** 9%; **Calcium:** 2%; **Iron:** 53%

Ingredients:

☐ *3/4 pounds ground beef*

- [ ] *5 ounces mushrooms, finely chopped*
- [ ] *3/4 pound ground pork*
- [ ] *1 large egg*
- [ ] *8 bacon slices*
- [ ] *3/4 teaspoon ground black pepper*
- [ ] *2/3 cup onion, finely minced*
- [ ] *2 teaspoons Worcestershire sauce*
- [ ] *2 teaspoons salt*
- [ ] *1 cup vegetable oil*
- [ ] *1/4 cup fresh parsley, minced*
- [ ] *1/3 cup ketchup, no sugar added*
- [ ] *1/2 cup pork rind crumbs*
- [ ] *1 tablespoon Dijon or brown mustard*
- [ ] *Non-stick cooking spray*

Directions:

1. Preheat the oven to 350F or 180F.

2. Grease the broiler rack with non-stick cooking spray.

3. Place a big, heavy skillet over medium heat. Pour in the oil. Put the onions and the mushrooms. Sauté until they are soft. Allow to cool for a couple of minutes.

4. Except for the bacon, put the rest of the ingredients in a big mixing bowl including the mushrooms. Blend well.

5. Pour the meatloaf mix into the greased broiler rack. Form it into a loaf 5–6 inches wide, 8–9 inches long, and 2 inches thick.

6. Lay the bacon slices diagonally over the loaf, tucking in the ends and along the side of the loaf.

7. Cut off the ends of any excess bacon.

8. Bake for about 90 minutes, or until the bacon is cooked and the loaf juices run clear.

9. Allow to stand for about 15 minutes. Slice, spoon the juices in the pan over the slices. Serve.

Zoodle Chicken Soup

This comforting, warm soup is great during cold days. Zoodles are also a great alternative for noodles.

Prep Time: 20 minutes **Cook Time:** 25 minutes

Serving Size: 562 g; **Serves:** 6; **Calories:** 394

Total Fat: 30.9 g **Saturated Fat**: 5.7 g; **Trans Fat**: 0 g

Protein: 20.9 g; **Net Carbs:** 7 g

Total Carbs: 9.3 g; **Dietary Fibre:** 2.3 g; **Sugars:** 4.7 g

Cholesterol: 32 mg; **Sodium**: 1170 mg; **Potassium**: 786 mg;

Vitamin A: 67%; **Vitamin C**: 34%; **Calcium**: 6%; **Iron**: 10%

Ingredients:

☐ *9 cups chicken broth*

☐ *3 zucchini, zoodled*

☐ *3 cloves garlic, minced*

☐ *2 tablespoons olive oil*

☐ *10 tablespoons vegetable oil*

☐ *1/2 teaspoon dried oregano*

☐ *1/2 teaspoon dried basil*

☐ *1/2 pound chicken breast, cooked, cut into bite-sized pieces*

☐ *1 cup sliced carrots*

☐ *1 cup diced onions*

☐ *1 cup diced celery*

- ☐ *Salt and pepper, to taste*
- ☐ *1 pinch dried thyme (optional)*

Directions:

1. In a large-sized pot, heat the olive oil over medium-high heat. Add the onion, garlic, and celery; sauté for about 5 minutes or until just tender.

2. Add the oil, chicken, and the carrots; sauté for 1 minute more. Add the broth, oregano, basil, thyme, and season with salt and pepper; bring to a boil. Reduce the heat to medium-low; simmer for about 20 minutes or until the vegetables are tender.

3. Divide the zoodles between six bowls; ladle the broth mixture over the zoodles.

Zoodle Carbonara

Using zoodles or zucchini noodles as an alternative for pasta in the traditional carbonara recipes makes this dish low carb. Omitting the cream also makes this dish gluten-free.

Prep Time: 15 minutes **Cook Time:** 5 minutes

Serving Size: 237 g; **Serves:** 2; **Calories:** 563

Total Fat: 46.4 g **Saturated Fat:** 15.5 g; **Trans Fat**: 0 g

Protein: 34 g; **Net Carbs:** 4.6 g

Total Carbs: 6.2 g; **Dietary Fibre:** 1.6 g; **Sugars:** 2.1 g

Cholesterol: 337 mg; **Sodium**: 1670 mg; **Potassium**: 512 mg;

Vitamin A: 24%; **Vitamin C:** 29%; **Calcium:** 40%; **Iron**: 13%

Ingredients:

☐ *2 ounces cubed pancetta, or to taste*

☐ *1 egg yolk*

☐ *1 zucchini, extra-large sized, cut into noodle-shape strands*

☐ *2 eggs*

☐ *2 tablespoons grated Parmigiano-Reggiano cheese*

☐ *2 tablespoons olive oil*

☐ *2 teaspoons ground black pepper*

☐ *2/3 cup shredded Pecorino cheese, or to taste*

Directions:

1. In a bowl, whisk the egg yolks and the eggs together. Add the pecorino cheese; mix well.

2. In a large wok or a skillet, heat the olive oil over medium heat. Add the pancetta, cook, stirring, for about 2-3 minutes or until cooked through, but not crispy.

3. Add the zoodles; cook, stirring, for about 3-5 minutes, or until the zoodles are warmed, but not soft, and the pancetta are slightly crisp. Remove the wok or the skillet from the heat.

4. Pour the egg mixture over the zucchini noodles; stir until evenly coated. Top the zoodles with the Parmigiano-Reggiano cheese and season with the black pepper.

Roast Chicken and Gravy

Have you ever tried cooking a whole chicken in a slow cooker and ended with the bird meat coming out stringy, dry, mushy, and overcooked? Then this recipe is just what you are looking for! The whole cooked chicken comes out amazing and moist. Make sure not to cook the bird longer than 6 hours on low. If there is any leftover gravy, be sure to save them. The gravy will be incredible on everything.

Prep Time: 20 minutes **Cook Time:** 4-6 hours

Serving Size: 376 g; **Serves:** 6; **Calories:** 597

Total Fat: 22 g **Saturated Fat**: 10.5 g; **Trans Fat:** 0 g

Protein: 88 g; **Net Carbs:** 4 g

Total Carbs: 4.9 g; **Dietary Fibre:** 0.9 g; **Sugars:** 1.8 g

Cholesterol: 266 mg; **Sodium:** 253 mg; **Potassium:** 651 mg;

Vitamin A: 9%; **Vitamin C:** 6%; **Calcium**: 6%; **Iron:** 16%

Ingredients:

- [ ] *6 garlic cloves, peeled*
- [ ] *4 pounds chicken, organic kosher*
- [ ] *6 tablespoons ghee*
- [ ] *2 onions, chopped medium*
- [ ] *1/4 cup white wine or extra chicken stock*
- [ ] *1/4 cup chicken stock*
- [ ] *1 teaspoon tomato paste (or up to 1 tablespoon)*
- [ ] *Freshly ground pepper*
- [ ] *Kosher salt*
- [ ] *Sunny Paris seasoning (or your preferred seasoning)*

Directions:

1. In a large cast-iron over medium heat, melt the ghee. Put in the onions and the garlic. Add in the tomato paste. Cook for about 8–10 until soft and lightly browned.

2. Pour in the wine to deglaze the pan. Transfer the mixture to the slow cooker.

3. Dry the chicken. Season well both the inside and outside with the salt, pepper, and your preferred seasoning. With the beast down, put the chicken into the slow cooker. Close the lid. Cook for about 4-6 hours on low. When the cooked, transfer the chicken to a serving plate; let rest for 20 minutes.

4. Defat the cooking liquid. Adjust the seasoning. Blend with an immersion blender. Serve with the chicken.

Corned Beef and Cabbage Crockpot Style

Here is an easy way to make corned beef and cabbage. This keto dish is super cheap and super easy to make. Just put everything in the crockpot and dinner is ready when you with almost no effort at all.

Prep Time: 20 minutes **Cook Time:** 8 hours

Serving Size: 581 g; **Serves:** 6; **Calories:** 805

Total Fat: 62.4 g **Saturated Fat:** 21.9 g; **Trans Fat:** 0 g

Protein: 47.1 g; **Net Carbs:** 8 g

Total Carbs: 13.4 g; **Dietary Fibre:** 5.4 g; **Sugars:** 7 g

Cholesterol: 208 mg; **Sodium:** 3154 mg; **Potassium:** 887 mg;

Vitamin A: 106%; **Vitamin C**: 100%; **Calcium**: 11%; **Iron**: 105%

Ingredients:

- ☐ *1 small onion*
- ☐ *1 celery bunch*
- ☐ *4 carrots*
- ☐ *4 cups water*
- ☐ *½ teaspoon ground coriander*
- ☐ *½ teaspoon ground mustard*
- ☐ *½ teaspoon black pepper*
- ☐ *½ teaspoon salt*
- ☐ *½ teaspoon allspice*
- ☐ *½ teaspoon ground marjoram*
- ☐ *½ teaspoon ground thyme*
- ☐ *5.88 pounds corned beef*
- ☐ *1 large head cabbage*

☐   *3/4 cup vegetable oil*

Directions:

1. Cut up the onions, celery and carrots and line the bottom of the crockpot.

2. Add 4 cups of water.

3. Mix all the spices; rub both sides of the corned beef with the spices and place on top of the vegetables

4. Cover and cook in the crockpot for 7 hours on low.

5. Clean cabbage, wash, and quarter.

6. Place the cabbage in the crockpot, add the oil, and cook for an additional 1 hour on low.

Chapter V

Pistachio-Crusted Sun-dried Tomato Goat Cheese Balls

These simple, quick-to-put-together little nibbles are deliciously creamy, tangy, and crunchy. They can be easily made for an impromptu gathering or a spur of the moment snack.

Prep Time: 10 minutes **Cook Time:** 0 minutes

Serving Size: 69 g (1 ball) g; **Serves:** 7 (1 ball each); **Calories:** 277

Total Fat: 21.6 g **Saturated Fat:** 12.5 g; **Trans Fat:** 0 g

Protein: 16.5 g; **Net Carbs:** 4.6 g

Total Carbs: 6 g; **Dietary Fibre:** 1.4 g; **Sugars:** 1.3 g

Cholesterol: 51 mg; **Sodium:** 257 mg; **Potassium:** 321 mg;

Vitamin A: 21%; **Vitamin C:** 27%; **Calcium:** 45%; **Iron:** 8%

Ingredients:

- [ ] *1 package (4 oz.) of sun-dried tomato*
- [ ] *12 ounces goat cheese*
- [ ] *½ cup de-shelled pistachios*
- [ ] *Salt to taste (sea salt is best)*

Directions:

1. Cut goat cheese into 7 slices and form into balls

2. Lightly crush pistachios (don't grind them)

3. Add salt to pistachio to taste

4. Roll cheese around in the pistachio mixture. Completely cover

5. Chill and enjoy.

Magical Mushroom Powder

If fish sauce is liquid umami in a bottle, this is powdered umami in a jar and an indispensable supply in your kitchen arsenal. Once you get a taste of how good food is with this powder, you'll want to sprinkle it on everything. You may even replace your salt and pepper with this. Sprinkle on your scrambled, pan-fried eggs, salad, on some avocado, or over your favorite meat dish.

Prep Time: 5 minutes **Cook Time:** 0 minutes

Serving Size: 1 g (more or less) g g; **Makes:** 1 1/4 cups; **Calories:** 1

Total Fat: 0 g **Saturated Fat:** 0 g; **Trans Fat:** 0 g

Protein: 0.1 g; **Net Carbs:** 0.1 g

Total Carbs: 0.1 g; **Dietary Fibre:** 0 g; **Sugars:** 0 g

Cholesterol: 0 mg; **Sodium:** 0 g; **Potassium:** 0 mg;

Vitamin A: 0%; **Vitamin C:** 0%; **Calcium:** 0%; **Iron:** 0%

Ingredients:

- ☐ *1 ounce dried porcini mushrooms*
- ☐ *1 tablespoon red pepper flakes*
- ☐ *1 teaspoon freshly ground black pepper*
- ☐ *2 teaspoons dried thyme*
- ☐ *2/3 cup kosher salt*

Directions:

1. In a clean spice grinder, pulse the dried mushrooms until finely ground.

2. Transfer the finely ground mushroom into a bowl.

3. Add the salt, thyme, pepper flakes, and pepper.

4. Mix thoroughly.

5. Store the mix in an airtight container. It will keep for several months.

Keto-Pieces (Peanut Butter Cups)

If you love Reese's Peanut Butter Cups, then you will love this homemade version. The taste is very similar, but these are low-carb. In fact, these cups can be considered "fat bombs" with high-fat content that will help you meet your daily fat need.

Prep Time: 5 minutes **Cook Time:** 5 minutes

Serving Size: 59 g; **Serves:** 4; **Calories:** 358

Total Fat: 37.5 g **Saturated Fat:** 20.2 g; **Trans Fat:** 0 g

Protein: 5.3 g; **Net Carbs:** 3.4 g

Total Carbs: 5.5 g; **Dietary Fibre:** 2.1 g; **Sugars:** 1.6 g

Cholesterol: 71 mg; **Sodium:** 241 g; **Potassium:** 175 mg;

Vitamin A: 16%; **Vitamin C:** 0%; **Calcium:** 2%; **Iron:** 15%

Ingredients:

- [ ] *1 stick of grass-fed butter*
- [ ] *1 ounce of raw unsweetened chocolate*
- [ ] *5 packets Stevia*
- [ ] *2 tablespoons heavy cream*
- [ ] *5 tablespoons of all natural peanut butter*

Directions:

1. Melt both the butter and chocolate in the microwave for about a minute (depending on your microwave)

2. In a bowl, mix the chocolate the melted chocolate and butter together.

3. Add 5 packets of Stevia to the butter and chocolate and mix.

4. Add 2 tablespoons of heavy cream and peanut butter and taste.

5. Line muffin tins with cupcake papers and adds in the chocolate mixture

6. Freeze until firm, serve and enjoy!

Brussels Sprouts Chips

Vegetable chips are the trend these days, and they are an absolute hit. I mean, who can resist them? This delicious version is crunchy and can rival potato chips any time of the day. This low carb salty snack is rich in vitamins A and C. These chips are vegan, gluten-free, and Paleo-friendly as well.

Prep Time: 5 minutes **Cook Time:** 8-10 minutes

Serving Size: 101 g; **Serves:** 2-4; **Calories:** 150

Total Fat: 13 g **Saturated Fat:** 8 g; **Trans Fat:** 0 g

Protein: 3 g; **Net Carbs:** 4.7 g

Total Carbs: 8 g; **Dietary Fibre:** 3.3 g; **Sugars:** 1.9 g

Cholesterol: 33 mg; **Sodium:** 100 g; **Potassium:** 343 mg;

Vitamin A: 21%; **Vitamin C:** 124%; **Calcium:** 3%; **Iron:** 6%

Ingredients:

- *2 cups Brussels sprout leaves (the outer leaves from 2 pounds of sprouts)*
- *2 tablespoons ghee, melted*
- *Kosher salt to taste*
- *Optional: Lemon zest*

Directions:

1. Preheat oven to 350F.

2. Line two large baking trays with parchment paper. Set aside.

3. In a large bowl, mix the Brussels sprouts, ghee, and the salt together.

4. Divide the leaves into two even sets. In a single layer, arrange into the prepared tray.

5. Bakes each tray for about 8 to 10 minutes or until the leaves are brown around the edges and crisp. Add lemon zest over the chips, if desired. Eat immediately.

Pizza Balls

You will love this pizza balls without the flour. It's a dream come true. These low-carb meatballs stuffed with cream cheese are economical, quick to make, and perfect as a high-fat snack, appetizer, breakfast, lunch, or dinner. You can even double or triple this recipe for the weeks ahead. They can be served warm, cold, with, or without dips. Plus, they are portable. You can carry them around as on the go munchies.

Prep Time: 15 minutes **Cook Time:** 0 minutes

Serving Size: 51 g (1 ball); **Serves:** 2-4 (2 balls each); **Calories:** 106

Total Fat: 9.9 g **Saturated Fat**: 4.6 g; **Trans Fat**: 0.2 g

Protein: 3.4 g; **Net Carbs:** 1.1 g

Total Carbs: 1.1 g; **Dietary Fibre:** 0 g; **Sugars:** 0 g

Cholesterol: 26 mg; **Sodium:** 244 g; **Potassium:** 73 mg;

Vitamin A: 5%; **Vitamin C**: 3%; **Calcium**: 2%; **Iron**: 3%

Ingredients:

- ☐ *14 slices pepperoni*
- ☐ *8 black olives, pitted*
- ☐ *4 ounces cream cheese*
- ☐ *2 tablespoons fresh basil, chopped*
- ☐ *2 tablespoons sun-dried tomato pesto*
- ☐ *Salt and pepper, to taste*

Directions:

1. Dice the olives and the pepperoni slices into small pieces.

2. In a mixing bowl, mix the cream cheese, pesto, and basil together.

3. Add the pepperoni and the olive in the cream cheese mixture. Mix to combine.

4. Form the mixture into balls. Garnish with olive, pepperoni, and basil.

Bacon Wrapped Scallops

The tender scallops and the crisp bacon nicely complement each other. The scallops are infused with the sweet, smoky flavor of the bacon. You can eat all of the 12 pieces yourself without any guilt since each piece is very low-carb.

Prep Time: 15 minutes **Cook Time:** 5 minutes

Serving Size: 42 g; **Serves:** 12 (1 wrap each); **Calories:** 107

Total Fat: 8.2 g **Saturated Fat**: 4.2 g; **Trans Fat:** 0 g

Protein: 7.4 g; **Net Carbs:** 0.8 g

Total Carbs: 0.8 g; **Dietary Fibre:** 0 g; **Sugars:** 0 g

Cholesterol: 31 mg; **Sodium:** 194 g; **Potassium:** 134 mg;

Vitamin A: 4%; **Vitamin C:** 2%; **Calcium:** 1%; **Iron:** 1%

Ingredients:

- [ ] *12 thin bacon slices*
- [ ] *12 scallops*

- ☐ *12 toothpicks*
- ☐ *Salt and pepper to taste*
- ☐ *2 dashes paprika*
- ☐ *5 tablespoons ghee or oil of choice*

Directions:

1. Heat a skillet over high heat.

2. Add 1 Tablespoon of oil.

3. Wrap each scallop with a piece of bacon and secure with a toothpick; season with salt and pepper.

4. Cook for 2.5 minutes per side.

5-layer Keto Dip

This low-carb dip is a version of the 7-layer bean dip minus the beans and the olives. Hence, this recipe is only 5 layers. Serve with fried keto-friendly pita as a chip or your favorite low-carb chips.

Prep Time: 10 minutes **Cook Time:** 10 minutes

Serving Size: 187 g; **Serves:** 10; **Calories:** 347

Total Fat: 34.2 g **Saturated Fat**: 13 g; **Trans Fat**: 0 g

Protein: 10.7 g; **Net Carbs:** 9.1 g

Total Carbs: 12.1 g; **Dietary Fibre**: 3 g; **Sugars:** 3.6 g

Cholesterol: 55 mg; **Sodium**: 749 g; **Potassium**: 241 mg;

Vitamin A: 17%; **Vitamin C**: 5%; **Calcium**: 26%; **Iron**: 4%

Ingredients:

☐ *20 ounces guacamole*

☐ *4 ounces cream cheese*

☐ *4 ounces mayonnaise*

☐ *8 ounces sour cream*

☐ *2 tablespoons taco seasoning*

☐ *16 ounces salsa*

☐ *10 ounces cheddar cheese, shredded*

☐ *4 ounces green onions, diced*

Directions:

1. Start by combining the cream cheese, mayo, sour cream and seasoning

2. Mix until smooth

3. Chop up the green onions

4. Using a medium sized casserole dish, start by spreading out the guacamole on the bottom

5. Then carefully spread the sour cream mixture over top of the guacamole

6. Now spread the salsa over the sour cream mixture

7. Add the cheese

8. Top with green onions

9. This dip tastes best if you let it rest for several hours; overnight is also good.

Marinated Mozzarella

These cubes look very festive and pretty. They can be made ahead of time; just chill in the refrigerator until ready to serve.

Prep Time: 15 minutes, plus marinating; **Cook Time:** 0 minutes

Serving Size: 55 g; **Serves:** 10; **Calories:** 188

Total Fat: 14.8 g **Saturated Fat:** 5.8 g; **Trans Fat:** 0 g

Protein: 13 g; **Net Carbs:** 1.8 g

Total Carbs: 1.8 g; **Dietary Fibre:** 0 g; **Sugars:** 0 g

Cholesterol: 24 mg; **Sodium:** 276 g; **Potassium:** 10 mg;

Vitamin A: 9%; **Vitamin C:** 1%; **Calcium:** 33%; **Iron:** 0%

Ingredients:

☐ *1/3 cup olive oil*

☐ *1 tablespoon sun-dried tomatoes, oil-packed, chopped*

☐ *1 tablespoon fresh parsley, minced*

☐ *1 teaspoon red pepper flakes, crushed*

☐ *1 teaspoon dried basil*

☐ *1 teaspoon chives, minced*

☐ *1/4 teaspoon garlic powder*

☐ *1 pound mozzarella cheese, cubed*

Directions:

1. In a large-sized re-sealable bag, except for the

mozzarella cubes, combine the rest of the ingredients, shaking to incorporate. Add the cubes, seal the bag, and turn, coating the cheese cubes.

2. Chill in the refrigerator for at least 30 minutes. Serve with toothpicks.

Baked Kale Chips

This recipe is another great potato chips alternative. These chips are low-carb and are Paleo-friendly. These delicious, salty, crunchy munchies are rich in vitamin C and A.

Prep Time: 13 minutes; **Cook Time:** 12 minutes

Serving Size: 137 g; **Serves:** 4; **Calories:** 208

Total Fat: 17 g **Saturated Fat**: 1.3 g; **Trans Fat**: 0 g

Protein: 3.4 g; **Net Carbs:** 1.8 g

Total Carbs: 12.5 g; **Dietary Fibre:** 1.9 g; **Sugars:** 0 g

Cholesterol: 0 mg; **Sodium:** 49 g; **Potassium:** 566 mg;

Vitamin A: 349%; **Vitamin C**: 233%; **Calcium:** 15%; **Iron**: 10%

Ingredients:

☐ *1 pound (2 large bunches) kale; wash, stem, and dry thoroughly (They must be super dry. Pat them dry with paper towel, if necessary.)*

- ☐ *5 tablespoons macadamia nut oil or your preferred fat*
- ☐ *Magical Mushroom Powder, Fleur de sel, or your choice of seasoning salt*
- ☐ *Optional: Zest of 1 small lemon, finely grated*

Directions:

1. Place the rack in the middle position of the oven.

2. Preheat oven to 350F. Line a couple of rimmed baking sheets parchment paper. Set aside.

3. Using your hands, toss the kale leaves with your preferred oil, coating the leaves evenly.

4. In a single layer with some distance between, arrange the leaves on the prepared baking sheets, making sure they are not folded over so they will bake properly. Bake for about 12 minutes or until the leaves are crisp but are not burnt.

5. Remove from the oven; season with your preferred seasoning and with the lemon zest, if desired.

Avocado Chicken Crackers

This healthy spread is quick to make. You can use salmon instead of chicken or leave out the meat entirely, and the spread would still taste great on your favorite low-carb crackers. If you add chopped jalapeños and tomatoes would make this spread like chicken guacamole.

Prep Time: 15 minutes; **Cook Time:** 0 minutes

Serving Size: 59 g; **Serves:** 6; **Calories:** 109

Total Fat: 9 g **Saturated Fat:** 2.8 g; **Trans Fat:** 0 g

Protein: 4.2 g; **Net Carbs:** 1.5 g

Total Carbs: 4 g; **Dietary Fibre:** 2.5 g; **Sugars:** 0.6 g

Cholesterol: 14 mg; **Sodium:** 10 g; **Potassium:** 202 mg;

Vitamin A: 2%; **Vitamin C:** 8%; **Calcium:** 1%; **Iron:** 2%

Ingredients:

- ☐ *1 avocado; peel, pit, and mash*
- ☐ *1/2 onion; dice*
- ☐ *1/2 cup cooked chicken, chopped or salmon*
- ☐ *1 tablespoon lime juice*
- ☐ *1/4 teaspoon garlic powder*
- ☐ *1 tablespoon ghee or any oil*
- ☐ *To taste: Salt and ground black pepper*

Directions:

1. In a bowl, mix all the ingredients together. Spread on your favorite low-carb crackers, bread, or toast.

Hot Chocolate Mexican Cookies

These savory, spicy cookies taste great. They taste delicious that no one would believe they are dairy-free, gluten-free and low-carb. These chocolaty snacks are very rich and have a hint of heat.

Prep Time: 15 minutes; **Cook Time:** 20 minutes

Serving Size: 45 g; **Serves:** 5; **Calories:** 184

Total Fat: 15.1 g **Saturated Fat:** 11.8 g; **Trans Fat:** 0 g

Protein: 2.7 g; **Net Carbs:** 1.5 g

Total Carbs: 10.3 g; **Dietary Fibre:** 2.3 g; **Sugars:** 7.4 g

Cholesterol: 56 mg; **Sodium**: 79 g; **Potassium**: 111 mg;

Vitamin A: 5%; **Vitamin C**: 2%; **Calcium**: 2%; **Iron**: 13%

Ingredients:

- ☐ *8 tablespoons unsweetened cocoa powder*
- ☐ *4 large eggs*
- ☐ *3/4 cup coconut flour*
- ☐ *3 tablespoons salted butter*
- ☐ *2 teaspoons vanilla*
- ☐ *2 1/2 teaspoons cinnamon*
- ☐ *1/4 teaspoon salt*
- ☐ *1/2 teaspoons cayenne pepper*
- ☐ *5 packets of Stevia*
- ☐ *1/2 cup coconut oil*
- ☐ *1 1/2 teaspoons chili powder*

Directions:

2. Preheat the oven to 350F.

3. Put the coconut flour into a mixing bowl.

4. Add the cocoa powder, cayenne pepper, chili powder, stevia, and salt. Mix all of the ingredients together.

5. In a microwavable container, put the butter and the coconut oil. Microwave for about 10–15 seconds until liquefied.

6. Add the eggs and the vanilla into the butter mixture. Whisk them together.

7. Add the butter mixture into the dry ingredients. Mix well until the dry ingredients are completely soaked with the wet ingredients. Knead together with your hands if you have to.

8. Grease a pan. With your hands, form the dough into cookies. Do not roll because the pieces will crumble.

9. Bake for about 12–15 minutes. The cookies will be soft when you take them out from the oven.

10. Let them cool for a couple of minutes. Enjoy with low-carb milk.

Cheesy Jalapeño Popper

I have only recently discovered these delicious poppers and feel robbed of all the years I could have enjoyed them. These poppers are so tasty that I have eaten them every day for about a week and still want more!

Prep Time: 30 minutes; **Cook Time:** 10 minutes

Serving Size: 30 g (1 ball); **Serves:** 4 (1 ball); **Calories:** 109

Total Fat: 9.4 g **Saturated Fat:** 5.3 g; **Trans Fat:** 0 g

Protein: 3.5 g; **Net Carbs:** 1.1 g

Total Carbs: 1.1 g; **Dietary Fibre:** 0 g; **Sugars:** 0 g

Cholesterol: 29 mg; **Sodium:** 173 g; **Potassium:** 64 mg;

Vitamin A: 7%; **Vitamin C:** 3%; **Calcium:** 2%; **Iron:** 2%

Ingredients:

- ☐ *3 slices bacon*
- ☐ *3 ounces cream cheese*
- ☐ *1/4 teaspoon onion powder*
- ☐ *1/4 teaspoon garlic powder*
- ☐ *1/2 teaspoon dried parsley*
- ☐ *1 piece medium jalapeño pepper*
- ☐ *Salt and pepper, to taste*

Directions:

1. In a pan, fry the slices of bacon until crisp. Remove the bacon from the pan, keeping the bacon grease for later use. Allow the bacon to cool.

2. De-seed the jalapeño pepper and then dice into small pieces.

3. In a mixing bowl, combine the jalapeño, cream cheese, and spiccs, seasoning with salt and pepper to taste.

4. Add the bacon fat into the cream cheese. Mix until a solid mixture is formed.

5. Crumble the crispy bacon and put on a plate.

6. With your hands, roll the cream cheese into balls and then roll each ball into the crumbled bacon.

Fried Mac and Cheese

Here's another great recipe made from our favorite trusty keto vegetable –cauliflower. Baking a low-carb version of this recipe does not turn out that great; it comes out a bit crispy on the top but is mush throughout. The solution? Fry them! You can also make the patties in bulk for amazing, handy snacks anytime.

Prep Time: 20 minutes; **Cook Time:** 30 minutes

Serving Size: 162 g; **Serves:** 4; **Calories:** 367

Total Fat: 31.7 g **Saturated Fat:** 12.2 g; **Trans Fat:** 0 g

Protein: 16.8 g; **Net Carbs:** 3.1 g

Total Carbs: 5.4 g; **Dietary Fibre:** 2.3 g; **Sugars:** 2.2 g

Cholesterol: 184 mg; **Sodium:** 336 g; **Potassium:** 333 mg;

Vitamin A: 24%; **Vitamin C:** 53%; **Calcium:** 35%; **Iron:** 10%

Ingredients:

- 1 1/2 cup shredded cheddar cheese
- 1 head cauliflower, cut into florets
- 1 teaspoon turmeric
- 2 teaspoons paprika
- 3 large eggs
- 3/4 teaspoon rosemary
- 1/4 cup cooking oil, plus more as needed

Directions:

1. Put the cauliflower into a processor. Pulse until consistency until rice grain in sizes. Put the

cauliflower rice into a microwavable bowl. Microwave for about 5–7 minutes.

2. Place the microwaved cauliflower rice into a clean kitchen towel, roll it up tightly and apply pressure, wringing out as much excess moisture as you can. The cauliflower will be mushed. Transfer to a bowl. Allow to cool to room temperature.

3. One at a time, crack the eggs into the cauliflower. This will ensure that your mixture does not get too watery.

4. Add the rosemary, turmeric, and the paprika. Mix well.

5. Add the cheese. With your hands, mix everything well.

6. In a skillet, pour and heat olive oil or coconut oil until very hot.

7. Form the cauliflower mixture into balls and then flatten them with your palm, making patties.

8. Put the cauliflower patties into the skillet. Reduce the heat to medium high.

9. Cook until the bottom side is crisp. Flip and continue cooking until the turned side is crisp.

Crispy Mushroom Chips

Even the pickiest eaters will find these chips very satisfying. This low carb crunchy, crispy snack is packed with umami flavor – not salty, not sweet, not bitter, and not sour. These chips are also a good source of potassium, which is important in low-carb diets.

Prep Time: 15 minutes; **Cook Time:** 45-60 minutes

Serving Size: 163 g; **Serves:** 2; **Calories:** 144

Total Fat: 13.2 g **Saturated Fat:** 7.9 g; **Trans Fat:** 0 g

Protein: 4.8 g; **Net Carbs:** 3.5 g

Total Carbs: 5 g; **Dietary Fibre:** 1.5 g; **Sugars:** 2.6 g

Cholesterol: 33 mg; **Sodium**: 86 g; **Potassium**: 478 mg;

Vitamin A: 8%; **Vitamin C**: 7%; **Calcium**: 0%; **Iron**: 24%

Ingredients:

- ☐ *300 grams (10 ounces) King oyster mushrooms*
- ☐ *2 tablespoons ghee, melted*
- ☐ *Kosher salt*
- ☐ *Freshly ground pepper*

Directions:

1. Preheat non-convection oven to 300F (275F for convection oven).

2. Line a couple of rimmed baking sheets with parchment paper. Set aside. You can choose to bake in several batches or use multiple trays.

3. Cut the mushrooms lengthwise into half. Cut the

253

mushrooms into 1/8-inch thin slices using a mandolin slicer. Brush melted ghee on both sides of the mushroom slices; season with salt and pepper.

4. In a single layer, arrange the slices on the prepared baking sheets, leaving some space between slices.

5. Bake for about 45-60 minutes or until the mushrooms are crispy and golden brown, making sure that you pull them out when they are crisp. They will not continue to crisp if you pull them out when they are still soft.

Chapter VI

Sample Meal Plan for a Week

It does not have to be a struggle to stay on your Ketogenic Diet. Use the recipes you find in this book and you can eat great food. Try this sample Ketogenic Diet for one week and you will find how easy it is to stick with the diet!

	Breakfast	*Lunch*	*Dinner*
Monday	Two fried eggs with 2 strips of bacon	Keto Taco Salad Top w/ sour cream and salsa	Lazy Keto Chicken Small salad w/ blue cheese
Tuesday	Keto Cereal w/Almond milk	Avocado Tuna Melt Bites	Sirloin steak with steamed or raw spinach.
Wednesday	Steak and eggs	Two hamburger patties with cheese and bacon.	Lasagna
Thursday	Protein Pancakes	Keto Pizza w/ small side salad	Herb Baked Salmon and Broccoli
Friday	Pesto & Feta Omelet	Chicken Chili Tomato soup w/sour cream garnish	Keto Breaded Chicken Parmesan and Zoodles

Saturday	Eggs Benedict	Ham and Cheese Keto Stromboli	BBQ Pork Ribs Small dinner salad
Sunday	Keto Lemon-Poppy Seed Muffins Scrambled eggs	Keto Italian Sub	Steak with Mushroom Port Sauce Steamed Veggies

The Ketogenic Diet has existed in many variations over the years. In fact, it may have been the first diet humans have ever known. But the real question is: "Should I go for it?" Hopefully, by this point, the answer is a no-brainer.

If you are still deciding if this diet is worth your time, the only question you should answer is "What do I have to lose?".

Making big changes in life is never easy. In fact, most people delay making changes until they need to.

If you're 25 and in shape, make a change, so you're not 45 and overweight. If you're 45 and overweight, make a change, so you're not 65 and diabetic. If you're 65 and diabetic, make a change so that you're still alive and healthy at 85! It's never too early, or too late to take control of your health.

The Ketogenic Diet is becoming more and more popular because it works. It is not a fad, and it is not a trend. Studies keep coming out that show the tremendous benefits of being on a low-carb, high-fat diet.

Even good ideas take time before mainstream culture recognizes its benefits. Take a car, for example. It is something today that is universally considered a pretty good idea. However, when it first came out, people thought it was too smelly, too loud and too dangerous. A horse drew carriage was considered to be a safer and more efficient mode of transportation!

There is a similar resistance to the idea of having a low carb diet. After all, fruits and vegetables are carbs! How can those be bad?

That is when scientific research come into play. It shows people on a Ketogenic Diet diet burn more fat per hour, and have lower blood pressure. It also shows people that are on it have an increase in good cholesterol and a decrease in bad cholesterol. With more and more research coming out there will be a point where the benefits of the diet are undeniable. So it is better to start your journey on the road to greater health today.

There will, of course, be some challenges along the way. For example, most people look at you strange when you tell them you're on a low-carb diet. You might as well be telling them that you entered a booger-eating contest and won first place! Because their reaction would be similar; half shock and half disgust.

If you want even more confusion, try telling a waiter that you're on a Ketogenic Diet, and you can't have sugar in your salad dressing.

I found the easiest thing to tell people is that you're not eating carbs because you're trying to be healthy. Also, tell the waiter you can't have any sugar because you're diabetic. Just make sure you know the difference between type 1 and type 2!

If you are just starting out, just know that you may feel lethargic and weak the first week or two when you begin the diet. But don't be alarmed, just know that this is your body changing to a fat burning machine!

When you first start the Ketogenic Diet, it is best to avoid strenuous exercise for the first week or so. To help kick-start your weight loss go for a nice long walk. If you go to the gym often, keep the weights light and focus on easy cardio. Adding MCT Oil will also help you give you more energy during this period. But the most important thing to do is just be patient and give your body time to adjust.

Remember to consume the majority of your calories from high-quality fats and protein. Treat yourself every now and again with fresh fruit or a glass of wine. Make sure to limit your carbohydrate intake to about 20 to 60 grams per day. Nevertheless, every person is different. Some people need to stay under 20 grams to enter ketosis. Others can go up to 80 grams and still get into ketosis. However, when starting out, keep carbs on the lower end.

If you are on the diet and become tempted to give up or have a really bad cheat meal, just focus on your priorities in life. Look at what you have achieved. Do you feel better? Are you losing weight? Remember that you are on the path to a better lifestyle.

When you have a setback, handle it immediately. If you eat or drink something that isn't on your diet, don't give up. The Ketogenic Diet is a lifestyle change. There will be occasions where you fall to temptation. When you eat a certain amount of carbs, you will come out of ketosis. Just be aware that it isn't the end of the world, and it may just take you a couple of days to get back into the flow. It is easy to get caught off track, but once you are on the diet and notice all the positive effects it will be easy to get back.

You can help stay motivated by getting support from other Ketogenic Dieters. I recommend going on Facebook and typing in Ketogenic. There are many fantastic groups you can join with people that will inspire you daily. You can also reach out to me on Twitter @JeremyStoneEat I would love to hear from you.

Just remember that the hardest part of this diet is the first few days. Once you get past that point, things get much easier. So think about your family, think about your friends, most importantly think about yourself, and never give up!

Thank you again for downloading this book. I hope this book was able to help you to start and stay on a Ketogenic Diet. The next step is just to get going!

Finally, if you enjoyed this book I'd like to ask you to leave a review for this book on Amazon, it would be greatly appreciated!

I am constantly looking for way to improve my content to give readers the best value so If you didn't like the book I would also like to hear from you:

Twitter: @JeremyStoneEat

Thank you and good luck!

CPSIA information can be obtained
at www.ICGtesting.com
Printed in the USA
LVOW04s1357310816

502655LV00017B/169/P